THE

Peach Truck®

COOKBOOK

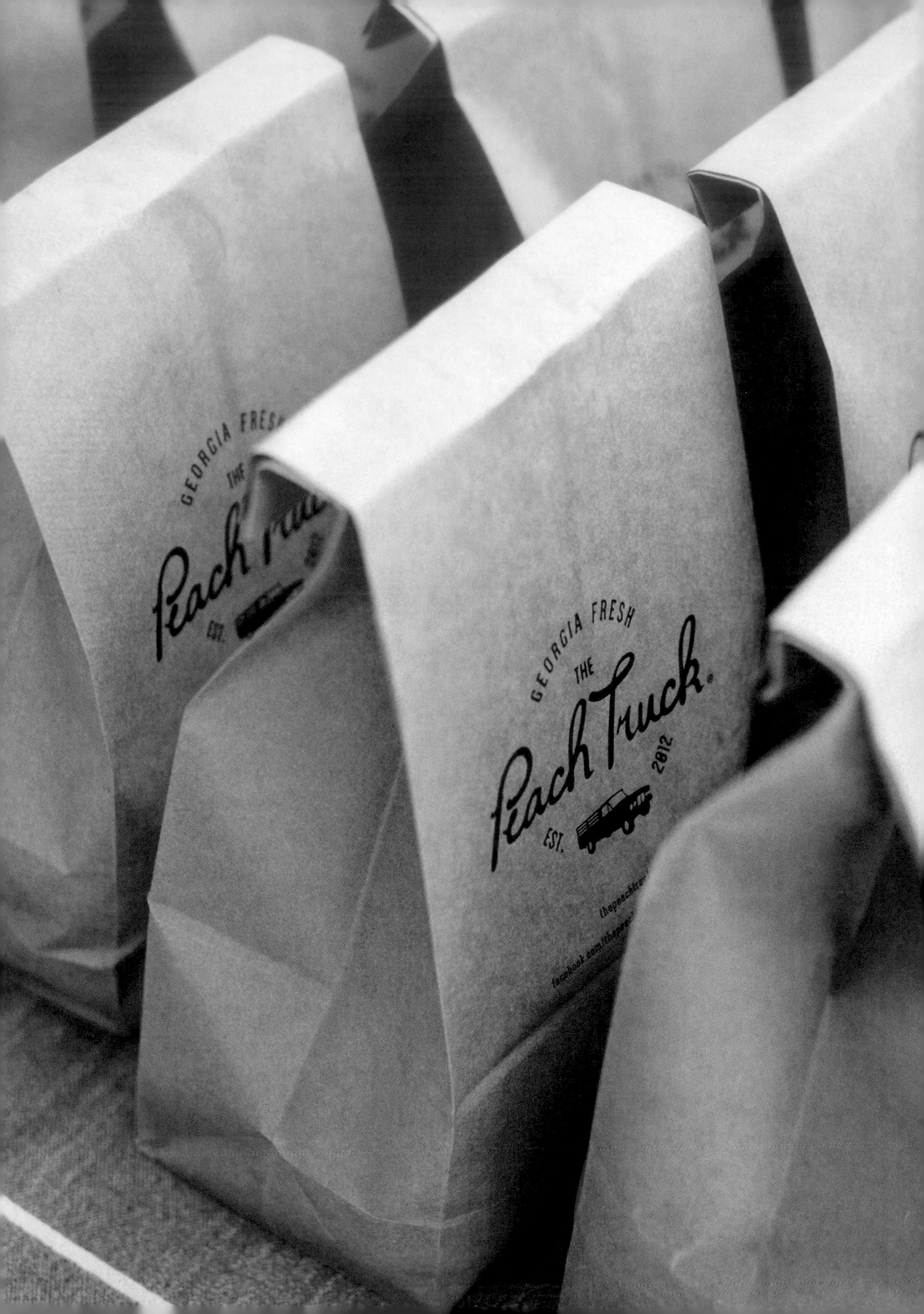
GEORGIA FRESH
THE
Peach Truck
EST.
2012

THE

Peach Truck®

COOKBOOK

100 DELICIOUS RECIPES FOR ALL THINGS PEACH

BY JESSICA N. ROSE & STEPHEN K. ROSE

PHOTOGRAPHS BY ELIESA JOHNSON

SCRIBNER

NEW YORK LONDON TORONTO SYDNEY NEW DELHI

Scribner
An Imprint of Simon & Schuster, Inc.
1230 Avenue of the Americas
New York, NY 10020

First Scribner hardcover edition June 2019

SCRIBNER and design are registered trademarks of The Gale Group, Inc.,
used under license by Simon & Schuster, Inc., the publisher of this work.

For information about special discounts for bulk purchases,
please contact Simon & Schuster Special Sales at 1-866-506-1949
or business@simonandschuster.com.

The Simon & Schuster Speakers Bureau can bring authors to your live event.
For more information or to book an event, contact the Simon & Schuster Speakers Bureau
at 1-866-248-3049 or visit our website at www.simonspeakers.com.

Interior design by Jen Wang
Photographs by Eliesa Johnson

Manufactured in the United States of America

3   5   7   9   10   8   6   4   2

Library of Congress Cataloging-in-Publication Data is available.

ISBN 978-1-5011-9267-8
ISBN 978-1-5011-9269-2 (ebook)

To Florence Evergreen, Wyatt Ellsworth, and Rainier Beckett, who throughout this process were emptying our cupboards and raiding the pantry in a pursuit of their own culinary masterpieces. Everything was delicious!

CONTENTS

OUR

STORY

Very few fruits elicit an emotional reaction quite like a peach. Its arrival signals summer, often considered the most adventurous, magical time of the year. The minute you bite into one—soft, aromatic, so juicy you practically have to eat it outside—you can't help but be fully engaged in the present moment and, at the same time, tuned into a rush of memories. For Jessica, it's the memory of hosing off our kids on our front porch in Nashville after peaches left them sticky with yellow pulp. For Stephen, it's snagging a few freshly picked fruits from the packing house for a bike ride in town with his brother, Michael. For both of us, it's the summer crowds lining up for The Peach Truck, a warming sight after the hard work and uncertainty of winter.

What has a peach meant to you? Perhaps you've given it as an offering: to parents celebrating a new baby, to teammates after a tough game, to colleagues after a successful launch, or to friends just arriving in town. Maybe you've used the sweet tokens as bartering chips with your children (or is that just us?), or as the finale to a well-run race or a lazy summer night. Peaches are ambassadors to moments of pure happiness, and an entire, brilliant season. We never dreamed we'd be so lucky that they would also give us a business and a life.

Before they became our livelihood, peaches were Stephen's first love. As a child in Fort Valley, Georgia, Stephen grew up in the heart of peach country, eating fresh peaches right off the tree. Southwest of Macon, located in the middle of the state, Fort Valley is a small town known for Blue Bird school buses, hundred-year-old pecan trees, porch sitting, and peaches. Its lush and leafy orchards have been nourished for hundreds of years by the region's ideal growing conditions: mineral-rich red clay, cold winters, and hot summers. Families there have known one another for generations, and Stephen's was lucky enough to receive boxes of fresh peaches from local growers every summer. No matter what else was on the menu, peaches played a starring role at Stephen's house: fresh and served whole on the porch in the summers, or frozen and baked into cobblers and crisps in the winter months. Delicious and abundant, peaches were a way of life.

Growing up in the Pacific Northwest with three brothers, Jessica may not have been raised among peach orchards, but she did spend her childhood outdoors: camping in the mountains, hiking Mount Rainier, and swimming at a simple beach on Lake Washington. Summer brought raspberries, cherries from the family tree, and blackberries picked during evening bike rides; fall provided the gift of apples from eastern Washington, and the annual ritual of gathering with friends and family around a cider press. Jessica can still remember cutting apples in her uncle's garage while everyone cheered on whichever cousin was spinning the handle on the oak barrel. Dipping her finger into the cider foam, Jessica felt the power of fruit to bring people together.

Having met while working together in our early twenties, we connected immediately. Despite our differences—Jessica, a direct Seattle-ite, and Stephen, a boisterous Georgian teeming with Southern pride—we formed a friendship. We soon began dating, and when a job opportunity in Nashville brought Stephen back to the South, we both decided to move there. In 2010 Nashville was simmering: everywhere we looked, young creatives, chefs, and food entrepreneurs were making a go of it, and the city truly felt like a place where one might be able to carve something out of one's own.

The Nashville that we moved to posed a conundrum: the culinary scene was exciting, and we loved the energy from food aficionados and restaurateurs. Yet Stephen couldn't help noticing that though it was only a six-hour drive from the best peaches in the world, a Nashville resident couldn't scare up a freshly picked peach anywhere. Instead of the juicy staples of Stephen's childhood, all we found were poorly handled, bland impostors picked before they were ripe and shipped thousands of miles to sit on shelves. Beneath their attractive blush-red exteriors, they were disappointingly mealy and dry.

Despite Nashville's peach problem, we loved our new city, and we began to think seriously about getting married and settling there. By then Jessica had her own cleaning and organizing business; Stephen was grinding it out at an office job in sales. As we started planning for our future, we dreamed of having the freedom to live on our own terms. Stephen believed in what he was selling but hated losing the entire day to a cubicle. Jessica grew up watching her father run his own landscaping business—something that gave him the flexibility to surprise her at school in his red-and-yellow ski outfit and pull her out of afternoon classes for a last-minute skiing expedition in the mountains. We wanted to travel and have time together, but how would we be able to do that? We kept returning to the idea of freedom: it meant working on projects that mattered to us, and having the ability to set our own schedule and experience more of the world.

A 2012 trip to Stephen's hometown gave us a serendipitous idea. There, between seeing the house Stephen grew up in and meeting his family and friends, Jessica tasted her first Georgia peach, right off the tree. She'd never known this kind of simple luxury, so one clearly wasn't enough: she ate a second, and a third, and smuggled six more peaches into her tote bag. In that moment she instantly understood that those peaches held the beauty and richness of an entire region.

During that same visit, we found ourselves sitting on a porch with good family friends, the McGehees. Fifth-generation peach growers at Pearson Farm, they got to talking with us about the difficulties of getting the perfect peach into people's hands, and we bemoaned our peach situation in Nashville. In the midst of that conversation, we had a thought: What if we could bring their heavenly peaches to Nashville? We would cut out the middleman, and customers could experience the fruit at peak freshness and maximum sweetness. There was no grand plan, no pursuit of a partnership or talk of paperwork. The Peach Truck was built from a conversation on a porch with family friends.

A few days later, we exchanged vows in a Nashville backyard with a small group of loved ones. After a quick honeymoon, we returned to Nashville, worked a normal workweek, and then picked up a tiny batch of peaches that had been transported from the farm. That Saturday morning, we loaded them into Stephen's '64 Jeep Gladiator and went out to sell peaches in Nashville.

The early days were clunky; we hadn't yet figured out how to communicate what we were offering to Nashville, and our audience was understandably wary. One of our earliest setups was during a Tuesday night Supper and Song event at the cult denim boutique Imogene + Willie. Jessica remembers the awkwardness of getting ready that night. "Where am I putting the peaches? On the hood of the truck? This is where all the cool kids come—are we cool? Are we making a good impression or is this completely embarrassing?" It was beyond hot that evening; everyone was eating tacos and asking, "What are you?" And we were honestly thinking, *We don't really know who we are*. We sold six bags of peaches.

Luckily, we quickly found our footing. First, we realized that peaches belong in daylight; no one wants to grocery shop at night. We set up at Imogene + Willie the following Saturday morning. From the beginning, aesthetics were important to us. We knew the experience of buying a peach was sensory—that people would smell the fruit before they saw us or them. We also knew that our peaches were pristine, and our customers would be able to trust us. Rather than have them cherry-pick through a pile, we decided to select the peaches ourselves and pack them in sturdy brown paper bags that would stand up straight and look streamlined and crisp on the Turkish towels that Jessica loves. We really wanted our setup to emanate warmth and polish. We knew we had an extraordinary product; everything else needed to rise to the same level. It was a thrill when those first customers returned the following week.

That first summer of 2012, we worked our regular jobs Monday to Friday, then spent the weekends setting up at markets, parking our truck next to Imogene + Willie, knocking on the doors of our favorite restaurants, and giving away peach after peach in an effort to build trust and create a community. We were shooting from the hip—devoted to making our peach-truck dream work and patching together plans and potential customers as we went. Those early days, coordinating the transportation of the peaches from the farm to Nashville sometimes felt like arranging a drug deal: the McGehees would find someone who happened to be driving through and we'd arrange to meet them anywhere. Once, we backed our truck into a grocery store parking lot while a man, passing through on a road trip with his daughter, unloaded peaches he'd tucked into his trailer. By midsummer, The Peach Truck was selling out at every location, and we knew we were onto something. By the time the next peach season kicked in, we had quit our jobs to work on our business full-time.

Today, our peaches are featured on the menus of Nashville's best restaurants, from City House to Husk. People from all over the city buy them every week, and we've shipped them to thousands of customers in forty-eight states. Every summer, the Peach Truck Tour visits more than a hundred towns throughout the Midwest and Northeast, selling peaches in half-bushel boxes to snaking lines of more than five hundred people. Along the way, we've added a daughter and twin boys, more staff, and countless supporters and friends throughout the South and, increasingly, across the country. Ours is a love story that began with peaches, but it's also about much more: an idea, a truck, a family, and a city. It's about the pride we feel in getting a natural delicacy, tended to for months by hardworking family farms, over the finish line to an exuberant and appreciative customer taking a bite.

With this cookbook, we hope to deepen the connection between peaches, our family, and you. As parents of young children, we think about how to eat seasonally and healthily (and—because we're working like crazy—realistically), and how to incorporate the fruits of our labor into our day-to-day routines. The recipes here were created with a farm-to-table approach, but because they accompany a chronicle of our family's experiences, they also tap into the classic tradition and rich history of Southern cuisine, as well as beloved memories from our own parents' kitchens. One of the joys of our work has been becoming a part of the dynamism of Nashville's food scene, so these recipes also reflect what's percolating in the city, and the way new neighborhoods, new ethnic influences, and new ideas about what people like to eat come together by way of a simple stone fruit.

Food creates memories, and the human stories behind the peaches are what keep us going—whether we hear our peaches have been sent to a loved one several states away or we see "The Peach Truck peaches" on the menu at a favorite local spot for lunch. We came in with the idea of solving a practical issue, but it's now about so much more. Needless to say, Nashville no longer has a peach problem.

Jessica Nkosi + Stephen

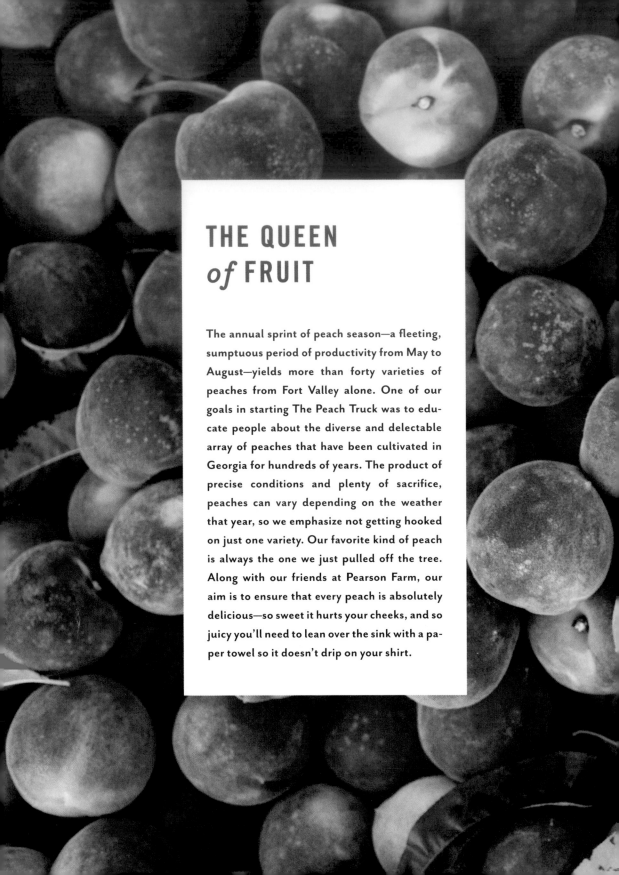

THE QUEEN
of FRUIT

The annual sprint of peach season—a fleeting, sumptuous period of productivity from May to August—yields more than forty varieties of peaches from Fort Valley alone. One of our goals in starting The Peach Truck was to educate people about the diverse and delectable array of peaches that have been cultivated in Georgia for hundreds of years. The product of precise conditions and plenty of sacrifice, peaches can vary depending on the weather that year, so we emphasize not getting hooked on just one variety. Our favorite kind of peach is always the one we just pulled off the tree. Along with our friends at Pearson Farm, our aim is to ensure that every peach is absolutely delicious—so sweet it hurts your cheeks, and so juicy you'll need to lean over the sink with a paper towel so it doesn't drip on your shirt.

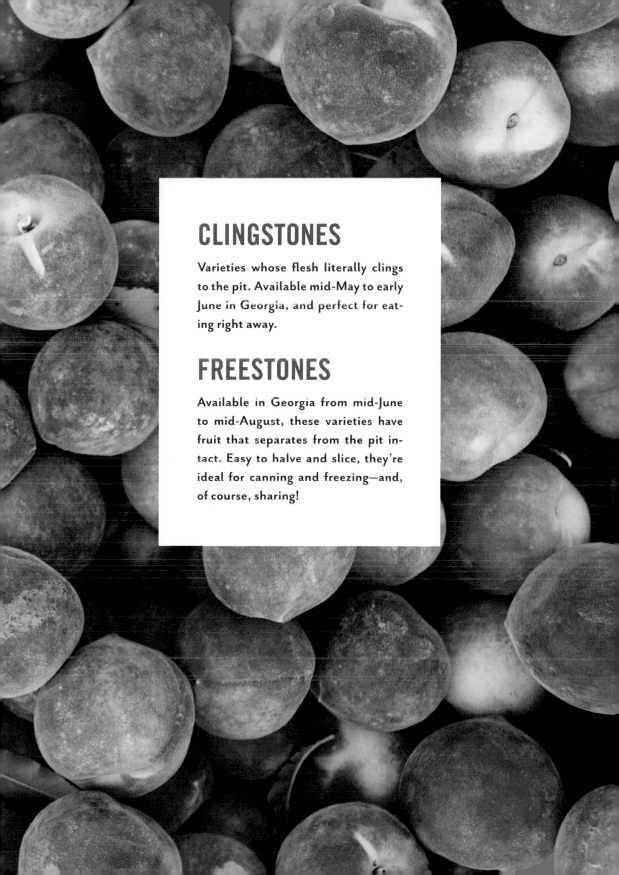

CLINGSTONES

Varieties whose flesh literally clings to the pit. Available mid-May to early June in Georgia, and perfect for eating right away.

FREESTONES

Available in Georgia from mid-June to mid-August, these varieties have fruit that separates from the pit intact. Easy to halve and slice, they're ideal for canning and freezing—and, of course, sharing!

A HISTORY OF
GEORGIA PEACHES

MID-1500S: Spanish monks in St. Augustine, Florida, introduce peaches to North America; the fruit soon spreads to islands along the Georgia coast.

MID-1700S: In the northern part of Georgia, Cherokee Indians begin to cultivate peaches.

MID-1800S: Peaches are shipped by steamship to New York City and other locations outside the South, where their reputation soon earns Georgia the moniker "The Peach State."

1870S: Georgia grower Samuel Henry Rumph crosses an Early Crawford peach with a Chinese clingstone variety and

creates an easy-to-ship, tender, yellow freestone peach with a memorable taste. He names it Elberta, after his wife. Thanks to the refrigerated train cars he invents in 1875, Rumph is able to transport his crops to northern states in unprecedented volumes.

LATE 1800S: The Georgia peach boom kicks off in Middle Georgia, with an influx of people arriving—gold rush–style—to grow peaches.

1885: Moses Winlock "Lockie" Pearson and his wife, Cornelia "Emma" Emory,

move to Fort Valley, in Crawford County, Georgia. They plant the first peach trees for what will become Pearson Farm.

1928: Expanded acreage results in an all-time high of nearly eight million bushels of Georgia peaches annually. The Elberta becomes synonymous with a Georgia peach.

2008: Pearson Farm, led by Al Pearson and son Lawton, enters its fifth generation.

2012: The Peach Truck is born!

WHAT IT TAKES
TO GROW A PEACH

Growing peaches requires attention, patience, perseverance, and heart. The best growers take care to focus on the quality of the harvest rather than obsess over the quantity at every step of the way. The simplicity of this truth has sustained us as we've built The Peach Truck. We could expand our business to many more locations, but the quality of our product would suffer, and quality is everything. It means we're sometimes sold out of peaches for a few days, but we'd rather have zero sales than pick a peach before it's ready. This truth shows itself equally to us in life, where we've found less to be more. The richness doesn't come from things—but from connectedness with our friends, our family, and each other.

MINERAL-RICH SOIL Georgia's red clay soil, which gets its color from iron oxides, nourishes peach groves.

450 TO 900 CHILL HOURS Peaches need to grow under the right conditions, having a delicate balance of enough chill hours each winter—under 45°F being optimum—without experiencing a late-spring freeze.

HOT, HUMID SUMMERS While several states grow peaches, we firmly believe that none can compete with the combination of Georgia's cool winters and its unmatched summer heat! Higher temperatures ripen Georgia peaches to an ideal level of sugar content.

CAREFUL PRUNING When the trees are dormant late in the winter, growers assess the branches individually, removing enough to create a bowl-like center of the tree. As the fruit comes in, this provides airflow and gives equal sunlight to each peach-laden branch throughout the day.

THINNING THE BRANCHES Once warm weather triggers the tree to put out a crop, growers thin the tiny peaches by hand to limit the yield. Rather than thousands of small, tasteless peaches, the goal is to concentrate the tree's resources into fewer, larger, juicier fruits.

TURNING OVER NEW SOIL Once a tree has matured—which takes about twenty years—if it was planted on virgin soil, growers dig it up to let the ground replenish for a generation, planting other crops like cotton or soybeans on the plot. After a new peach tree is planted, it takes three to four years for it to yield a substantial crop.

VARIETIES

Pearson Farm cultivates more than forty varieties of peaches, and there's nothing we love more than getting them into the hands of joyful people all summer long. As we mentioned before, the best peach is the one in your hand, but here are a few to note.

- **FLAVORICH:** The first peaches off the tree in Georgia each year, the Flavorich's arrival in mid-May signals the beginnings of peach season. Dark red and medium-size, Flavoriches are more sugary than acidic, which makes them ideal for ambrosial and addictive peach preserves and jams.

- **FIESTA GEM:** If you ever get your hands on Fiesta Gems, stock up on as many as you can! Appearing early in June, the orange-red orbs have plumlike sweet-and-sour notes and are like natural SweeTarts. We like them in a medley of fresh fruit for color and zip or sliced and fanned in a beautiful French-style dessert tart.

- **HARVESTER:** Arriving in late June, Harvester peaches are the first to pull clean from the pit, and there's no turning back to clingstones from there! They're extra juicy, ready to enjoy right away, even right off the tree, or to save for colder climes by canning or freezing, their summer goodness ready to burst forth in winter-baked peach muffins or pies.

- **FLAME PRINCE:** These tangy-sweet beauties—named for their fiery crimson tones—come out in early August and produce for about ten days. A first-rate snack just as they are, they are also great in a salad or a peach syrup that has a little kick.

- **ELBERTA:** The peach that made Georgia famous, these freestones come from some of the most active trees, which can produce up to 150 pounds in one season. As modern agribusiness has evolved and grocery stores increasingly seek consistent color and a long shelf life, the Elberta—a fuzzy, bright yellow variety—has seen decreased demand. This is a shame! People tend to think they look like they were picked too early, but it's not true. They're one of the sweetest varieties, perfect for canning, drying, baking in pies and cobblers, or being eaten as is.

BREAK

FAST

A GOOD START

The Peach Truck began with us chasing an idea, came together through hard work and complicated logistics, and is at its best when it adds flavor and goodwill to our community; but it is ultimately only as successful as the quality of the product in our truck. Our peaches are unparalleled in taste and delectableness because they've been picked—often just twenty-four hours before—by family operated farms in Georgia, who bring intuition, thoughtfulness, and institutional knowledge to the practice of growing peaches. While it forever holds the distinction of being dubbed the Peach State, Georgia actually is not the state that produces the most peaches (that honor goes to California). But even though others grow more, we strongly believe that none can claim to grow *better* peaches year after year. According to the USDA, eighty million pounds of peaches come out of Georgia in a typical year, the vast majority of which, in a contrast to other states, are generated by these small family operated farms.

In 2019, an operation like Pearson Farm, which grows most of our peaches, feels special. For 134 years, ever since Lockie Pearson and his wife, Emma, planted their first peach trees in a plot of red clay soil, Pearson Farm has been specializing in the fruit. The four generations that have followed have been careful to balance innovation with tradition. While the property has grown to eighteen hundred acres (and now includes additional acreage for pecans), it still relies on good old human taste buds, more than high-tech sugar-testing tools, to make decisions, and they still do everything—from pruning trees to thinning out young peaches to picking mature fruit—by hand. Since peaches are so delicate, no machine could treat their tender fruit with the sensitivity they require.

We've learned a lot about sustainability from the Pearsons, both professionally and personally. The first generation of growers in their family could have easily gotten every last nutrient out of the soil, but their approach has always been about the long game: Rotate the crops; plant trees you'll never harvest so that future generations can; think about yourself, but also your extended family, your kids and their eventual families. Focus on creating something that will endure, and you'll be able to weather the unpredictability of each individual peach season year after year.

Stephen grew up running around with Pearson and McGehee kids in the orchards, and Jessica was enamored the first time she saw the farm, driving past the property's original white farmhouse, hundred-year-old pecan trees, and rows of ripe peach trees about to bear fruit. Through working with the Pearsons, we've had the pleasure of sharing their story with countless new customers and educating them about the taste, not just the look, of great peaches, and we were honored when they relayed to us their gratitude for the human connection we've helped put back into peach growing.

Mornings start early at Pearson Farm: around 5:45 each day from February to August. Like every peach operation in Georgia, Pearson undergoes the same seasonal cycle of harvesting the crop: mowing, fertilizing, pruning, thinning, and picking. The farm is proud of the fact that they have a high retention rate among their workers. Now working with second- and third-generation families, Pearson views their workers as professionals, and they invest in them, which comes through in the care and quality of their operation. As owner and grower Lawton Pearson says, "The real crux of the peaches is the people."

Our own days during peach season start early and hectic. Jessica is a breakfast person; she needs a minute to prep for the day. In an ideal world, this would include a cup of hot coffee and an egg taco with sriracha, although with three toddlers, that doesn't always happen. Meanwhile, Stephen is fueled mostly by insane amounts of coffee, with the occasional slice of toast eaten on the run.

But in spite of our frenzied weekday mornings, we are a family with an affinity for breakfast food, even if the time we're most likely to get around to it is Sunday brunch. Stephen especially loves the sweet-and-savory contrasts of a brunch menu. Involve fried chicken, and that's how you'll get him to the breakfast table.

So a good start is important to us—it's the foundation of our business. And to start the day with a peach—does anything sound better? Whether baked into a fluffy pancake, sautéed and spooned onto grits, or simply sliced fresh and added to your bowl of cereal, peaches offer a dose of beauty and brightness, even before the sun comes up. No matter what time of day you enjoy them, the recipes here—toasted granola, sweet grits, buttermilk pancakes with caramelized peaches (!!)—we hope you'll savor the natural sweetness as you head into whatever your day holds.

The Georgia Açai Bowl

Açai bowls are healthy, look beautiful, and—most important—are an excellent way to get kids to eat chia seeds. They feel like summer in a bowl. One of our favorite versions in Nashville is the "Southern" at Franklin Juice, which is topped with peaches and pecans. In our version, you can make the most of whatever fruit you have on hand: we like to add ¾ cup sliced banana, but yours might include flaxseeds or hemp seeds, protein powder, or a dollop of nut butter or yogurt. We recommend keeping sliced strawberries, bananas, and peaches in the freezer for easy assembly in the morning.

Serves 1
Hands-on time: 6 minutes
Total time: 6 minutes

1 peach, pitted and sliced (1¼ cups)

2 (4-ounce) packets frozen unsweetened açai puree

1 tablespoon honey

¾ cup sliced banana

¾ cup sliced strawberries

1 tablespoon chia seeds

1 tablespoon unsweetened coconut flakes

1 teaspoon bee pollen

1. Set aside ¼ cup of the peach slices. Place the remaining peach slices in a food processor. Break up the açai slightly and place in the food processor with the peach slices. Add the honey, ½ cup of the banana, and ½ cup of the strawberries. Blend until smooth and thick.

2. Spoon into a bowl and arrange the reserved ¼ cup peach slices, remaining ¼ cup banana slices, remaining ¼ cup strawberry slices, the chia seeds, and the coconut flakes on top. Sprinkle with the bee pollen and serve.

Peach Dutch Baby

Light and fluffy, this popover-pancake hybrid fares best in a cast-iron skillet heated in the oven that will ensure the batter puffs up properly. Once it gets baking, this baby will rise impressively and then quickly collapse. We love to serve it warm, with berries added to the peach slices on top, or at room temperature, as a sweet afternoon snack.

Serves 4
Hands-on time: 10 minutes
Total time: 45 minutes

5 tablespoons unsalted butter

1 cup chopped peaches (about 1 medium)

4 tablespoons granulated sugar

3 large eggs

¾ cup whole milk

¾ cup all-purpose flour

½ teaspoon kosher salt

TO SERVE

3 tablespoons powdered sugar

2 cups sliced peaches, about 2 medium (optional)

1. Preheat the oven to 425°F.

2. Melt 1 tablespoon of the butter in a 10-inch cast-iron skillet over medium-high heat. Add the chopped peaches and 1 tablespoon of the granulated sugar and cook, stirring often, until the peaches begin to brown, about 3 minutes. Remove the peaches from the skillet and wipe the skillet clean. Place the skillet in the hot oven for 10 minutes.

3. Blend the eggs, milk, flour, remaining 3 tablespoons granulated sugar, and the salt in a blender until smooth.

4. Add the remaining 4 tablespoons butter to the skillet and swirl the skillet until the butter has melted. Pour the batter over the melted butter in the skillet without mixing it in. Spoon the caramelized peaches on top of the batter. Transfer the skillet to the oven and bake for 20 to 25 minutes, until puffed and golden.

5. Serve immediately, topped with a dusting of powdered sugar and additional sliced peaches, if desired.

The Buckwheat Stack

Stephen is always on the lookout for a good pancake—a habit that goes back to the Saturday mornings of his childhood when his dad, an expert hotcake flipper, would make breakfast for the whole family.

Now that we have a little family of our own, Stephen has kept up with this tradition and is always trying to take his pancake game to the next level. This recipe further hones his craft: the rich sweetness of the peaches and the whipped mascarpone turn the everyday buckwheat batter into a decadent weekend affair. You can take care of steps 1 and 2 the night before: cover and chill the peaches, then let them come to room temperature or warm them by sautéing quickly before using. We like the color contrast of blueberries here, but cherries, raspberries, or strawberries would work well, too.

*Makes 12 pancakes and 1½
cups mascarpone cream*

Hands-on time: 30 minutes

Total time: 30 minutes

MASCARPONE CREAM

½ cup mascarpone cheese (4 ounces)

6 tablespoons powdered sugar

Pinch of kosher salt

1½ teaspoons pure vanilla extract

½ cup heavy cream

PEACHES

2 tablespoons unsalted butter

2 cups chopped peaches (about 2 medium)

1 tablespoon granulated sugar

2 tablespoons molasses

1. To make the mascarpone cream, whisk together the mascarpone, powdered sugar, salt, and vanilla in a large bowl until smooth. Beat the cream with a handheld mixer on medium speed until soft peaks form. Whisk about one-third of the whipped cream into the mascarpone. Gently fold in the remaining whipped cream. Do not overmix.

2. To make the peaches, melt the butter in a medium skillet over medium-high heat. Add the peaches and granulated sugar; cook for 4 minutes, or until beginning to brown. Add the molasses; cook for 1 minute, or until syrupy. Transfer to a plate to cool.

3. To make the pancakes, whisk together both flours, the baking soda, baking powder, granulated sugar, and salt in a large bowl. In a separate bowl, whisk together the egg yolks, buttermilk, and melted butter. In a clean bowl, whisk or beat the egg whites with a handheld mixer until stiff peaks form. Add the buttermilk mixture, beaten egg whites, and peaches (with any juices that have collected on the plate) to the flour mixture; fold until just combined (there will be lumps).

PANCAKES

1½ cups all-purpose flour

½ cup buckwheat flour

½ teaspoon baking soda

1 teaspoon baking powder

2 tablespoons granulated
   sugar

1 teaspoon kosher salt

2 large eggs, separated

1½ cups buttermilk

4 tablespoons (½ stick)
   unsalted butter, melted

Vegetable oil, for greasing

TO SERVE

1½ cups fresh berries

Maple syrup

4. Heat a griddle or large skillet over medium-high heat. Lightly brush the surface with vegetable oil. Working in batches, pour ⅓ cup of batter per pancake onto the hot griddle and cook until small bubbles form on the surface of the pancakes and the bottoms are golden brown, about 2 minutes. Flip the pancakes and cook for 1 minute, or until browned on the bottom and cooked through.

5. Serve the pancakes immediately, topped with the whipped mascarpone cream, fresh berries, and maple syrup.

Peach Candied Bacon

Early in our marriage, we got into Benton's bacon—a local favorite that's thick and so deliciously smoky the scent lingers in the house a day after you cook it. The beauty of this recipe is that it takes any regular bacon and ups the ante. You can do so much with it! Add it to scrambled eggs, crumble it over a green salad, sprinkle it across French toast, slide it into a sandwich, or add it to a Bloody Mary. It's a flavorful secret weapon.

Makes about 10 slices
Hands-on time: 30 minutes
Total time: 30 minutes

1 pound thick-cut applewood-smoked bacon

½ cup The Peach Truck Signature Peach Jam (page 263)

2 tablespoons light brown sugar

⅛ teaspoon cayenne pepper

1. Preheat the oven to 425°F. Line a large rimmed baking sheet with aluminum foil.

2. Arrange the bacon slices in a single layer on the prepared baking sheet. Bake for 15 to 20 minutes, until the bacon is beginning to brown but not completely cooked through. Remove from the oven and drain the fat from the baking sheet; keep the oven on.

3. Combine the jam, brown sugar, and cayenne in a small saucepan. Bring to a boil over medium-high heat; reduce the heat to medium and cook, stirring constantly, for 2 minutes.

4. Brush both sides of the bacon with the jam mixture. Return it to the oven and bake for 5 to 7 minutes more, until browned, bubbling, and crisp. Remove from the baking sheet and let cool for 10 to 15 minutes on a wire rack before serving. Store at room temperature for up to 4 hours.

Sweet Sorghum Grits

Jessica will be the first to tell you she didn't grow up a grits person, but after learning a different way of making them, she quickly changed her mind. The key to this version is a technique from culinary legend and Husk founder Sean Brock, who divulged in his cookbook, *Heritage*, that to bring out the best texture and flavor of grits, one must soak them overnight. Not only will they cook faster, but they'll have a heavenly, creamy consistency. Soak your grits, people! We promise you'll feel like you're getting away with something. Sorghum syrup provides the best balance of sweetness, but you can substitute honey. If you don't have hemp seeds, throw in finely chopped toasted nuts of your choice for some welcome crunch.

*Makes 4 cups grits and
2 cups sorghum-peach mixture;
serves 4*

Hands-on time: 35 minutes

Total time: 8 hours 35 minutes

1 cup stone-ground grits

2 cups whole milk

1 teaspoon kosher salt

2 tablespoons sugar

6 tablespoons (¾ stick) salted butter

¼ cup sorghum syrup

2½ cups sliced peaches (about 3 large)

¼ cup hemp seeds

⅛ teaspoon ground cinnamon

1. Stir together the grits and 2½ cups water in a medium bowl. Cover and let stand at room temperature for 8 hours or up to overnight.

2. Bring the milk to a simmer in a large heavy saucepan over medium-high heat. Add the salt and sugar. Slowly pour the grits and their soaking liquid into the pot. Stir and return to a boil. Reduce the heat to medium-low and cook, stirring often, until the grits are thick, tender, and creamy, about 30 minutes. Stir in 4 tablespoons of the butter.

3. Melt the remaining 2 tablespoons butter in a medium skillet over medium-high heat. Stir in the sorghum syrup and peaches; reduce the heat to medium-low and simmer, stirring occasionally, for 3 minutes, or until the peaches are softened.

4. Stir together the hemp seeds and cinnamon in a small bowl.

5. Divide the grits evenly among four bowls and top each with the peaches and the pan juices. Sprinkle the cinnamon hemp seeds over the top.

Peach Almond Streusel Muffins

Good news! The streusel for these crumbly, buttery breakfast treats can be made up to one day ahead and kept in the refrigerator. More good news! These muffins are best the day they're made, so don't hold back if you'd like to eat one . . . or three.

Makes 12 muffins
Hands-on time: 12 minutes
Total time: 42 minutes

ALMOND STREUSEL

3 tablespoons all-purpose flour

¼ cup almond meal

3 tablespoons granulated sugar

2 tablespoons cold unsalted butter, cut into pieces

MUFFINS

2¼ cups all-purpose flour

1 teaspoon baking powder

½ teaspoon baking soda

½ teaspoon kosher salt

½ teaspoon ground cinnamon

½ teaspoon ground ginger

1 cup packed light brown sugar

6 tablespoons vegetable oil

⅔ cup buttermilk

1 large egg

½ teaspoon pure almond extract

1½ cups chopped peaches (about 1 large)

¼ cup sliced almonds, toasted

1. Preheat the oven to 375°F. Line a 12-cup muffin tin with paper liners.

2. To make the streusel, whisk together the flour, almond meal, and granulated sugar in a medium bowl. Add the butter and work it into the flour mixture with a pastry blender or your fingertips until the mixture resembles small peas. Cover and chill while you prepare the batter.

3. To make the muffins, whisk together the flour, baking powder, baking soda, salt, cinnamon, ginger, and brown sugar in a large bowl.

4. Whisk together the vegetable oil, buttermilk, egg, and almond extract in a medium bowl. Stir the wet mixture into the dry mixture until just combined. The mixture will be thick. Stir in the peaches.

5. Spoon the batter into the prepared muffin cups, filling them almost to the top. Sprinkle the almonds evenly over the top of each muffin, followed by about 1 tablespoon of the streusel.

6. Bake for 24 to 26 minutes, until the edges are golden brown and a pick inserted into the center of a muffin comes out clean. After baking, be sure to remove the muffins from the pan after 5 minutes so that they don't dry out. They'll keep at room temperature in an airtight container for 1 or 2 days—if they last that long.

Fried Chicken and Waffles

with Peach Compote

Jessica, who lived in Los Angeles during college, remembers thinking, *I have to have it*, when she heard about Roscoe's House of Chicken and Waffles, the beloved LA institution founded by a Harlem transplant and known for its signature, classically Southern dishes. What she experienced the first time she visited the establishment felt like something larger than a meal. It was a story, a family, a history, and a future wrapped up in a mouthwatering dish.

For this take on the traditionally Southern dish, marinate the chicken in the buttermilk and hot sauce for at least one hour—overnight is even better, if you have the time—to tenderize the meat, providing flavor and a subtle heat. If you prefer a more savory spin on your chicken and waffles, serve this dish with melted salted butter or Savory Peach Butter (page 256) instead.

Serves 4

Hands-on time:
1 hour 5 minutes

Total time:
2 hours 5 minutes

COMPOTE

1 pound peaches, pitted and coarsely chopped (about 3 medium)

¼ cup honey

1 tablespoon white balsamic vinegar

½ teaspoon ground cinnamon

¼ teaspoon freshly grated nutmeg

Pinch of kosher salt

Pinch of cayenne pepper

1. To make the compote, combine the peaches, honey, vinegar, cinnamon, nutmeg, salt, and cayenne in a small skillet or saucepan. Bring to a simmer over medium-high heat. Reduce the heat to medium-low and simmer, stirring occasionally, until thick and syrupy, about 5 minutes. Set aside.

(recipe continues)

CHICKEN

2 cups buttermilk

½ cup hot sauce

4 bone-in, skin-on chicken thighs (1½ pounds total)

4 skin-on chicken drumsticks (1¼ pounds total)

2 cups all-purpose flour

2 teaspoons kosher salt

1½ teaspoons garlic powder

1 teaspoon freshly ground black pepper

Vegetable oil, for frying

WAFFLES

1⅓ cups all-purpose flour

¾ teaspoon baking powder

½ teaspoon baking soda

¾ teaspoon kosher salt

2 teaspoons sugar

2 large eggs, separated

1¾ cups buttermilk

3 tablespoons unsalted butter, melted

TO SERVE

Maple syrup

Sweet Peach Butter (page 256)

2. To make the chicken, combine the buttermilk and hot sauce in a large bowl. Add the chicken and toss to coat. Cover and chill for at least 1 hour or up to overnight.

3. Whisk together the flour, salt, garlic powder, and black pepper in a large bowl. Drain the chicken, discarding the marinade. Toss the chicken, a few pieces at a time, in the flour mixture, coating each piece well and shaking off any excess flour. Let the chicken rest while the vegetable oil is heating (this helps form the crust).

4. Preheat the oven to 250°F. Set a wire rack over a rimmed baking sheet.

5. Fill a large Dutch oven or heavy deep skillet with the vegetable oil to a depth of 3 inches. Heat the oil over medium-high heat to 350°F. Working in batches, fry the chicken, turning occasionally, for 12 to 15 minutes, until cooked through. Drain the chicken on the wire rack and season with salt. Keep the chicken warm in the oven while you prepare the waffles.

6. To make the waffles, heat a Belgian waffle iron to medium.

7. Whisk together the flour, baking powder, baking soda, salt, and sugar in a medium bowl. Whisk together the egg yolks, buttermilk, and melted butter in a separate bowl. Beat the egg whites in a third bowl with a handheld mixer until stiff peaks form. Gently stir the buttermilk mixture and the beaten egg whites into the dry ingredients until just combined. Don't mind the lumps! You don't want to overmix the batter.

8. Pour ¾ cup of the batter into the waffle iron, spreading it to cover the plates. Close the waffle iron and cook until the waffles are browned and crisp and the steaming has stopped, about 4 minutes. Transfer the waffle to a platter. Repeat with the remaining batter.

9. Place one waffle on each of four plates. Top each with one chicken thigh and one drumstick. Serve with the compote, maple syrup, and a pat of homemade peach butter.

The Ultimate Sticky Bun

Doesn't your mouth water just reading this recipe? The dough, which you can make a day ahead, is going to be as buttery and soft as it sounds, so work quickly to roll and cut it as soon as it's ready. Ideally you'll let the dough rise overnight so the flavor really has time to sink in, but if you don't have time, just make sure your dough is cooled. You may find that as you add the soft butter to the dough, it will separate into shaggy pieces—just keep mixing! It will hang together once the butter is incorporated.

These are our new favorite Christmas sticky buns, and if you'd like to make them during the peach off-season, too, simply replace the filling with ¾ cup The Peach Truck Signature Peach Jam (see page 263) and sprinkle the tops with cinnamon and chopped pecans.

Makes 9 buns
Hands-on time: 37 minutes
Total time: 3 hours 37 minutes, plus overnight chilling

DOUGH

2½ cups all-purpose flour, plus more for dusting

1¾ teaspoons rapid-rise yeast

¼ cup granulated sugar

1 teaspoon kosher salt

2 large eggs, at room temperature

½ cup whole milk, warmed to 105° to 110°F

½ cup (1 stick) unsalted butter, cut into ½-inch pieces, at room temperature

1. To make the dough, whisk together the flour and yeast in the bowl of a stand mixer fitted with the dough hook. Add the granulated sugar, salt, eggs, and milk and mix on medium-low speed until the dough is well combined, about 3 minutes, scraping down the sides of the bowl as needed to incorporate the flour. Gradually add the butter, a few pieces at a time, scraping down the sides as needed and waiting until each addition of butter is incorporated before adding more. (The dough may start to look separated—this is okay, just keep mixing.) Once all the butter has been added, increase the speed to medium-high and mix for 5 minutes. Cover the dough and let rise at room temperature for 1 hour, or until doubled in volume. Punch down the dough and form it into a ball. Cover and refrigerate overnight.

(recipe continues)

FILLING

3 cups chopped peaches
(about 1 pound)

3 tablespoons granulated
sugar

½ teaspoon lemon zest

1 tablespoon fresh lemon
juice

½ teaspoon kosher salt

½ teaspoon ground
cinnamon

2. To make the filling, lightly grease a 9-inch square baking pan.

3. Combine the peaches, granulated sugar, lemon zest, lemon juice, and salt in a medium saucepan. Cook over medium-high heat until the peaches begin to break down, about 5 minutes. Mash the peaches with a potato masher. Cook for 3 minutes more, or until thickened. Stir in the cinnamon. Let cool completely. (The filling can be refrigerated overnight.)

4. To make the glaze, melt the butter in a medium saucepan over medium-high heat. Whisk in the brown sugar, honey, and salt and bring to a boil. Remove from the heat; whisk in the vanilla. Pour the glaze over the bottom of the prepared baking pan. Sprinkle the coarsely chopped pecans over the glaze.

5. Roll the dough out on a lightly floured surface into a 16 x 12-inch rectangle. Spread the filling over the dough, leaving a 1-inch border on the long side farthest from you. Sprinkle the filling with the finely chopped pecans. Starting with the long side closest to you, roll the dough up as tightly as possible. Pinch the seams to seal. Place the dough log seam side down. Cut the log crosswise into 9 equal pieces. Place the pieces cut side up in the prepared pan. Cover and let rise for 45 minutes to 1 hour, until doubled in size.

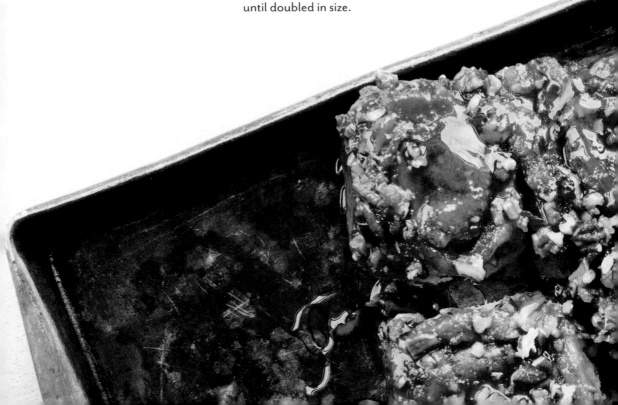

GLAZE

9 tablespoons unsalted butter

1 cup packed light brown sugar

1½ tablespoons honey

¼ teaspoon kosher salt

¾ teaspoon pure vanilla extract

¾ cup coarsely chopped pecans, lightly toasted

¼ cup finely chopped pecans, lightly toasted

6.   While the dough is rising, preheat the oven to 350°F and position the racks in the center and lower third. Line a baking sheet with aluminum foil.

7.   Place the buns on the rack in the center of the oven. Place the prepared baking sheet on the rack under the buns to catch any syrupy drips. Bake for 50 minutes, shielding the buns with foil after 40 minutes to prevent overbrowning, or until golden brown, bubbling, and a pick inserted into the center of a bun comes out clean. Run a knife along the edges of the pan to loosen the buns. Invert the pan onto a serving platter or large plate; wait for 10 minutes before removing the pan and serving.

Ginger Peach Smoothie

Since peach season is so fleeting, we try to freeze and can as many peaches as possible so we can enjoy our favorite fruit throughout the year. They most frequently pop up during the off-season in smoothies. We love packing the blender with healthy ingredients that give us a burst of morning energy and make our kids feel like they're getting a treat. If you prefer yours a little sweeter, you can add a couple more dates, a tablespoon of honey, or a generous splash of sweetened almond milk. If dairy's not your thing, substitute coconut yogurt for regular yogurt to achieve a similar consistency.

Serves 1
Hands-on time: 5 minutes
Total time: 5 minutes

1½ cups frozen sliced peaches

2 pitted dates, chopped

1 cup unsweetened almond milk

½ cup plain yogurt

1 teaspoon flaxseeds

½ ripe banana, sliced (about ½ cup)

½ teaspoon finely chopped fresh ginger

1 tablespoon honey

Pinch of kosher salt

Combine the peaches, dates, almond milk, yogurt, flaxseeds, banana, ginger, honey, and salt in a blender and process until smooth.

Not Your Basic Granola

Home-baked granola tastes leaps and bounds better than anything boxed, not to mention being much healthier—but have you tried making it with peaches? It's a wonderful way to add a sweet hint of summer to the usual mix of dried fruit and nuts. We love having it on hand for rushed breakfasts. Another good thing about granola is that you can use any nut you think will pair well with your ingredients—we like pecans, almonds, and hazelnuts. And if you don't care for cherries, try dried apricots, goji berries, or golden raisins.

Serves 10

Hands-on time: 40 minutes

*Total time: 40 minutes,
plus cooling time*

4 cups rolled oats

**2 cups unsweetened coconut
flakes**

**1 cup coarsely chopped
walnuts**

**½ cup honey or sorghum
syrup**

⅓ cup salted butter, melted

1 teaspoon ground cinnamon

½ teaspoon kosher salt

**1 cup chopped Dried Peaches
(page 267)**

1 cup dried cherries

1.   Preheat the oven to 350°F. Line a large baking sheet with parchment paper.

2.   Combine the oats, coconut flakes, and walnuts in a large bowl. Whisk together the honey, melted butter, cinnamon, and salt in a small bowl. Drizzle the honey mixture over the oat mixture. Toss to coat the oat mixture with the honey and butter.

3.   Spread the mixture evenly over the prepared baking sheet. Bake on the center rack for 30 minutes, or until deep golden brown, stirring every 10 minutes. Let cool.

4.   Store in airtight containers at room temperature for up to 1 week. Stir in the peaches and cherries just before serving.

THE PEACH TRUCK COOKBOOK

Rose Kids' Baked Oatmeal

Baked in a casserole, this was a quick, healthy, go-to meal in the early days with newborns. Jessica's friends JoAnna and Mallory are both known for their oatmeal bakes, and Jessica decided to put her own spin on it. As the kids have grown, oatmeal has become a staple in our home, especially served warm, with a dollop of yogurt for added calcium, or made ahead and cut into bars for a lunchtime snack.

Serves 12
Hands-on time: 10 minutes
Total time: 1 hour

3 large eggs

3½ cups whole milk

1 cup honey, plus more for topping

1 teaspoon pure vanilla extract

1 teaspoon kosher salt

½ teaspoon baking powder

8 cups old-fashioned oats

½ cup chia seeds

½ cup hemp seeds

3½ cups mixed fresh blueberries, blackberries, and raspberries

1½ cups diced peaches (about 1 large)

1. Preheat the oven to 375°F. Lightly grease a 13 x 9-inch baking pan.

2. Whisk together the eggs, milk, honey, vanilla, salt, and baking powder in a large bowl. Stir in the oats, chia seeds, hemp seeds, 3 cups of the berries, and the peaches. Pour into the prepared baking pan. Top with the remaining ½ cup berries. Bake for 50 minutes, or until the edges are golden brown and the center is set.

3. Serve warm or at room temperature.

Peach Coffee Cake

If you're getting ready to host a festive brunch or would like to serve breakfast with a little added gusto, this peach coffee cake is a definite crowd-pleaser. If you bring one next time you're headed over to friends, we guarantee you'll be invited back! The best part is you can make it the day before and keep it covered at room temperature. And please don't feel restricted by the pecans in the streusel—any kind of nuts will do, or you can even skip the nuts altogether. Just be sure to arrange the peaches in an even layer so that you get some peachy goodness in every bite.

Makes one 9-inch coffee cake

Hands-on time: 30 minutes

Total time: 3 hours 30 minutes

PECAN STREUSEL

¾ cup all-purpose flour

1 cup pecans, chopped

½ cup firmly packed light brown sugar

¼ cup granulated sugar

1 teaspoon ground cinnamon

1 teaspoon ground cardamom

1 teaspoon kosher salt

½ cup (1 stick) cold unsalted butter, cut into small pieces

CAKE

1½ cups all-purpose flour

¾ cup granulated sugar

2 teaspoons baking powder

½ teaspoon ground cardamom

1 large egg

4 tablespoons (½ stick) unsalted butter, melted

¾ cup heavy cream

2 teaspoons pure vanilla extract

2 or 3 medium peaches, pitted and cut into 8 wedges each

1. Preheat the oven to 350°F. Grease a 9-inch springform pan, lightly dust it with flour, and tap out any excess.

2. To make the streusel, combine the flour, pecans, brown sugar, granulated sugar, cinnamon, cardamom, salt, and butter in a large bowl and, using your fingers or a pastry blender, cut in the butter until the mixture has a sandy texture. Set aside.

3. To make the cake, sift together the flour, granulated sugar, baking powder, and cardamom. In a separate bowl, beat the egg, melted butter, cream, and vanilla using a handheld mixer or whisk until frothy. Fold in the flour mixture until smooth and blended. Do not overmix.

4. Transfer the batter to the prepared pan and smooth the top. Arrange the peaches evenly over the top of the batter, pressing them into the batter just a bit. Cover the top evenly with the streusel and pat it down.

5. Bake on the center rack for 1 hour, or until a pick inserted into the center of the cake comes out clean.

6. Place the cake on a wire rack to cool completely before removing it from the pan and serving.

HOW TO
PRUNE A PEACH TREE

Reducing the number of branches in a deliberate manner allows more sunlight and nutrients to reach each individual fruit, increasing its size and sugar content.

Prune trees in late winter after the last cold snap and just before the buds begin to break (in Georgia, this takes place between mid-February and mid-March).

Identify three to four main "scaffold" branches that can be used to create the V-shape of the tree.

Start about twenty-four inches off the ground by removing other large branches—especially any that are weak, interfering, or sloping downward—from the tree with loppers or a pruning saw. The scaffold branches and shoots that remain should have unobstructed access to sunlight.

The remaining three to four main branches should form a bowl-like center of the tree, so that a beach ball could be held comfortably in the center.

After you've cut the excess branches, shorten the rest by about one-third with pruning shears.

The trees will blossom with pink flowers and then put out leaves before yielding peaches in mid-May.

RESOURCE GUIDE FOR
FORT VALLEY, GEORGIA

Though small, Fort Valley is a mighty agricultural hub in the heart of peach country, with a character all its own. Visit in the summer, and you can go orchard-hopping and stop by the Georgia Peach Festival to taste the world's largest peach cobbler. In the fall, attention turns from peaches to football, where kids who spent summers packing peaches return to play on the championship Peach County High School football team. Whenever we're there, we relish the stillness of the farm and the pace of small-town life. We also make sure to drop in on these gems, some of which Stephen has been visiting since childhood.

TAPATIO MEXICAN RESTAURANT
We never pass through town without stopping at this authentic Mexican restaurant and ordering the *molcajete*, a carved stone bowl filled with grilled cactus, fresh radishes, chorizo, jalapeño, queso fresco, and hot salsa—all ready for rolling into a warm tortilla.

THE RAILROAD CAFE
Home of our favorite breakfast in town, the

Railroad Cafe is housed in a historic train station and has an extensive, unpretentious menu filled with Southern home cooking. Anything they serve for breakfast hits the spot—particularly the omelets, grits, and fresh-from-the-oven biscuits.

NU-WAY WEINERS

You won't find a better hot dog than the ones at this middle Georgia chain, where you can enjoy all the classic fixings, from chili to tater tots to pickles. Order the chili cheese hot dog and a drink with their famous flaky ice, and live it up!

YODER'S DEITSCH HAUS

When Stephen was a kid, his family would drive thirty minutes to the town of Montezuma to eat at Yoder's Deitsch Haus. It is worth the trip. The cafeteria-style comfort food is out of this world—piled-high plates of okra, mashed potatoes, butter beans, fried chicken, and chocolate pie. Afterward, head to the bakery next door and take a fresh loaf of bread or a homemade peanut butter pie to go.

PEARSON FARM

Between its storied history and lively agricultural operation, Pearson Farm has become an attraction in itself. Visit the packing house—converted from an old circa-1904 schoolhouse—where you can watch the peaches roll by on a conveyor belt as they're inspected and carefully packed. Don't leave before tasting the homemade peach ice cream and the farm's famous toasted pecans, another beloved Georgia specialty.

SMALL

BITES

CHASING A DREAM

From the minute we decided to quit our jobs in 2013 and work on The Peach Truck full-time, we knew we were in for a challenge. Roadside fruit selling happens all over the world, and you can ask anyone manning the booth what an exhausting, physical, strategically demanding business it is. In a way, one of the best assets we had on our hands was naivete—we didn't know how difficult it would be to pull the whole thing off, so we just dove right in. And it was hard. Very, *very* hard. In the summer of our second season, we were working seven days a week, averaging fourteen-hour days, and sweating it out in the Nashville heat as we tried to make our way into as many local communities as possible. At the same time, we were cobbling together the beginnings of what would become an annual hundred-city peach tour. We were showing up at farmers' markets, concerts, the back doors of restaurants, and random street corners, insisting people try our peaches and raving that they'd just been picked the day before.

One way in which we were fortunate: we were selling something that made for an excellent snack. Whether driving the five and a half hours from Fort Valley to Nashville, standing in the sun chatting up skeptical customers, realizing how little we knew about the trucking industry, or managing a team for the first time and fearing we'd miss our projections and not make payroll, we frequently relied on the refreshing, instantaneous pick-me-up of a peach.

An ideal source of fiber, vitamin A, and potassium, as well as a burst of natural sugar, peaches are a fantastic quick bite, and they—quite literally—kept us going. But less tangible things sustained us as well. The first was the desire to prove to ourselves that we had what it took to build our dream.

Jessica was rather painfully reminded of this reality one day, early on in our second Peach Truck summer, when she found herself slinging peaches at one of our local stops, the Food Co. The day had started off rainy, so she'd worn rain boots. Within a few hours, the rain stopped and the Tennessee sun and humidity came out in full force. Her shins, throbbing in the rubber boots from the sticky air, felt like they were on fire. In pain, and with a touch of heatstroke, she took off her boots and became a shoeless peach saleswoman. If we came across the booth setup today, it would receive a failing grade: Jessica was hot, tired, over the peaches, and barefoot. Of course, at that very moment, a white Cadillac pulled up and an older woman rolled down her tinted window. Jessica immediately smelled a rosy scent reminiscent of her great-grandmother's home in Galveston, Texas, and reverted to the best behavior of her ten-year-old self. The woman appeared concerned.

"Honey, what are you doing?" she inquired.

"Selling peaches . . ." I said, but when I tried to go into my spiel, she cut me off.

"But your husband—what does he do?"

"This, also."

"No—you both have other jobs, right?"

"No, this is all we do."

"Oh, sugar, no. No, no, no."

Almost in slow motion, she put on her oversized sunglasses, shifted her car into gear, and drove off.

At the time, she didn't crush Jessica's dreams—in fact, Jessica laughed. But she did make Jessica want to work harder. We still think about that woman. Is she a regular at our Food Co. stop today? Does she continue to pass the booth and wonder what "real" jobs we ended up finding? Either way, we are grateful for the fuel that early skeptic gave us to keep going.

The good stories of what we were putting into our community sustained us, too. In one Nashville neighborhood where fresh produce is scarce, Jessica gave ripe peaches to a group of kids who claimed they'd never had one before. One little boy took a bite, and his eyes got so big he didn't seem to mind that there was a river of juice running down his arm. He proceeded to ask for about nine more. No matter how many times we've witnessed it, there is nothing like seeing a child's first taste of a peach.

One early summer, during a brief moment when we came up for air, we were taken aback when someone posted on social media: "You know it's summer when The Peach Truck signs start popping up around town." That we could be part of ushering people into the most carefree time of year, synonymous with friends, family, and good food, felt incredible. Those small, memorable moments are like the recipes in this chapter—playful, nourishing, and energized by the simple, refreshing goodness of a peach.

NUTRITIONAL FACTS

- Peaches are a good source of fiber (2 mg), potassium (230 mg), and vitamins A and C.

- A medium peach has about 60 calories. Peach flesh and skin contain the antioxidant chlorogenic acid, which helps protect against free radicals.

- One medium peach is about the size of a daily recommended serving of fruit.

Peach Caprese Salad

In our house, mozzarella is a summertime indulgence, a treat we buy to go with the cherry tomatoes we grow in our garden. Tennessee grows great tomatoes, and when they're lined up with fresh peaches and just-picked basil, we're reminded of how great it feels to eat seasonally. The dressing can be made a day ahead, and for maximum stun factor, slice the peaches, tomatoes, and cheese into rounds.

Serves 4
Hands-on time: 10 minutes
Total time: 10 minutes

2 tablespoons balsamic vinegar

2 tablespoons fresh lemon juice

1 tablespoon stone-ground mustard

1 tablespoon honey

1 tablespoon chopped shallot

¾ teaspoon kosher salt

½ teaspoon freshly ground black pepper

¼ cup extra-virgin olive oil

½ pound mozzarella cheese, sliced

2 large peaches, sliced into rounds

2 medium heirloom tomatoes, sliced

Small handful of fresh basil leaves

Flaky sea salt

1. Whisk together the vinegar, lemon juice, mustard, honey, shallot, kosher salt, and pepper in a small bowl. While whisking, slowly drizzle in the olive oil and whisk until the dressing is emulsified.

2. Arrange the mozzarella, peaches, tomatoes, and basil on a serving platter or individual plates. Drizzle with the dressing, sprinkle with the sea salt, and serve.

Pickled Peach Deviled Eggs

In our experience, if you're a deviled-egg person, you never eat just one: you have to be stopped from devouring a dozen. Consider yourself warned: these are addictive. The chopped Pickled Peaches (which are insanely good on their own) take the place of the more traditional relish, for a bright, flavorful take on the classic Southern entertaining staple. You can cook the eggs up to two days beforehand, and they can be filled, covered, and chilled several hours before serving, leaving you time to get party ready.

Makes 24
Hands-on time: 24 minutes
Total time: 40 minutes

12 large eggs

⅓ cup mayonnaise

2 tablespoons Dijon mustard

1 tablespoon fresh lemon juice

1 tablespoon chopped fresh chives

3 slices bacon, cooked and finely crumbled

2 tablespoons minced Pickled Peaches (page 272)

Pinch of kosher salt

Pinch of freshly ground black pepper

GARNISH

24 thin slices Pickled Peaches

Sweet paprika

Microgreens or chopped fresh chives

1. Bring a large pot of water to a boil. Fill a large bowl with ice and water and set it nearby. Carefully lower the eggs into the boiling water. Cook for 12 minutes. Remove the eggs from the water and place them in the ice water to cool.

2. Peel the eggs and cut them in half lengthwise. Scoop out the yolks and transfer them to a medium bowl; set the whites aside on a platter. Mash the yolks with a potato masher. Add the mayonnaise, mustard, lemon juice, chives, bacon, minced pickled peaches, salt, and pepper and stir until smooth.

3. Spoon or pipe the egg yolk filling into the egg whites. Top each egg with a pickled peach slice, a dusting of paprika, and a sprinkling of microgreens.

Grilled Wings

with Peach Bourbon BBQ Sauce

The Peach Bourbon BBQ Sauce elevates this classic bar snack. So brush the sauce generously onto these wings! A simple, easy party snack that's great for kicking off festivities or bringing to a friend's potluck, these aren't spicy like traditional wings, but they are insanely good, and you can still serve them with ranch dressing, carrots, celery, and cold beer. And if you miss the heat, just add a few tablespoons of our Peach Hot Sauce (page 271) to the marinade.

Makes about 27 wings
Hands-on time: 20 minutes
Total time: 20 minutes

4 pounds chicken wings

¼ cup olive oil

1 tablespoon kosher salt

1 teaspoon freshly ground black pepper

1 cup Peach Bourbon BBQ Sauce (page 255)

1. Heat a grill to medium (400°F) or heat a grill pan over medium-high heat.

2. Toss the chicken wings with olive oil, salt, and pepper in a large bowl, coating them well. Put ⅔ cup of the BBQ sauce in a small bowl for brushing over the wings and set aside the remainder in a separate small bowl for serving.

3. Grill the wings, turning them occasionally, for 15 minutes, or until the skin is crisp and the wings are almost cooked through. Brush with BBQ sauce and grill for 5 minutes more.

4. Serve the wings warm, with the reserved BBQ sauce on the side.

Peachy Cheese Plate

We love finding new ways to bring peaches to the table or, in this case, the cheese plate. Served three ways—sliced, pickled, and preserved—the peaches' natural sugars pair beautifully with the rich creaminess of all types of cheese, from Brie to Gorgonzola to Manchego. The best part is that you can use whatever's at hand, and customize the plate to your and your guests' likes and dislikes. We love including homemade pimento cheese, another Southern classic, which can be made up to a week ahead. Kids can help with assembly, too.

Serves 8
Hands-on time: 10 minutes
Total time: 10 minutes

1 cup Pimento Cheese (recipe follows)

6 ounces assorted cheeses, such as Gorgonzola, aged Gouda, and Manchego

½ cup Marcona almonds

2 tablespoons raw honey

1 cup Pickled Peaches (page 272)

¼ cup The Peach Truck Signature Peach Jam (page 263)

1 tablespoon coarse-grain mustard

Crackers and sliced baguette, for serving

1 medium peach, pitted and thinly sliced (about 1 cup)

Place the cheeses evenly on a cheese board or platter, arranging small bowls of almonds, honey, pickled peaches, and jam around them. Add a dollop of mustard to the board. Fill out the board with crackers and slices of baguette and fresh peach slices.

PIMENTO CHEESE

Makes about 3 cups • Hands-on time: 5 minutes • Total time: 5 minutes

½ cup mayonnaise

¼ teaspoon freshly ground black pepper

2 ounces cream cheese, at room temperature

1 (4-ounce) jar diced pimentos, drained

8 ounces white cheddar cheese, grated

8 ounces extra sharp cheddar cheese, grated

1 green onion, chopped

Stir together all the ingredients in a medium bowl until smooth. Cover and chill until ready to serve. Store, covered, in the refrigerator for up to 1 week.

Snapper Peach Crudo

Crudo is an Italian specialty—a way of showing off the freshest catch with the subtlest of flavors. Here we combine summer bounty—a thinly sliced snapper, ripe peaches and two types of melon, a pinch of Fresno chile, and a splash of lemon juice—to create a perfect summer-evening bite. We recommend buying the freshest, highest-quality fish you can find—and feel free to substitute other fish, such as sea bass, striped bass, or sole, if it suits you. Thinly slicing the fish can sometimes seem daunting, but if we can do it, we know that you can! The best way to master it here is to keep the fish very cold—you should put it in the freezer for twenty minutes before starting—and use an incredibly sharp knife.

Serves 8
Hands-on time: 10 minutes
Total time: 10 minutes

¼ cup finely diced watermelon

¼ cup finely diced honeydew

½ small Fresno chile, seeded and minced (about 1 tablespoon)

3 tablespoons extra-virgin olive oil

2 tablespoons fresh lemon juice

1 small peach, pitted and sliced into ¼-inch-thick slices

½ pound skinless sashimi-grade snapper fillet, bones removed

Microgreens or fresh cilantro leaves

Pinch of ground sumac

Flaky sea salt

1 Toss together the watermelon, honeydew, chile, olive oil, and lemon juice in a large bowl. Arrange the peach slices on a platter or individual serving plates.

2. Cut the snapper fillet in half lengthwise, then slice it against the grain into ¼-inch-thick pieces. Top the peach slices with the snapper slices. Top the snapper with the watermelon mixture, drizzling any accumulated juices from the bowl over the top.

3. Garnish with microgreens, sumac, and salt. Serve immediately.

Grilled Peach and Shishito Peppers

This is summer simplicity at its best: smoky flavor from the grill, fresh herbs and peppers, salt, and a sweet peach finish. There are so many incredible flavors happening here that it makes us want to kick off our shoes and drink a cold glass of rosé. Feel free to use a grill pan if venturing outdoors isn't in the cards for you, and use a grill basket for the peppers if you don't have time to skewer each one individually. Sometimes we'll grill a steak medium-rare alongside the peppers, and presto, dinner is done.

Serves 8

Hands-on time: 15 minutes

Total time: 15 minutes

4 large peaches, pitted and cut into wedges

2 cups shishito peppers (6 ounces)

4 tablespoons olive oil

2 tablespoons fresh lemon juice

¼ cup chopped fresh parsley

¼ cup chopped fresh chives

¼ teaspoon freshly ground black pepper

1 teaspoon smoked sea salt

1. Heat a grill to medium (400°F) or heat a grill pan over medium-high heat.

2. Toss the peaches and shishito peppers with 2 tablespoons of the olive oil in a large bowl. Thread the peaches and peppers onto separate skewers.

3. Grill the shishito peppers for 5 to 6 minutes, until charred. Grill the peaches for 1 to 2 minutes, until grill marks appear. Remove the peaches and peppers from the skewers and transfer them to a large bowl. Add the remaining 2 tablespoons olive oil, the lemon juice, parsley, chives, and black pepper and toss to combine. Sprinkle with the salt and serve.

Stone Fruit Crostini

This snack has a savory base, which allows the natural sweet flavor of the cherry and peach to come through. Fresh, pretty, and heaped with summer's bounty, it's a wonderful way to kick off an evening, especially accompanied by a beautiful cocktail or a good glass of wine. We always think an enticing snack served early at a party is a sign that things are only going to get better as the night goes on.

A good-quality baguette will go a long way here, so pick one up from your local bakery. Cherries are our favorite accompaniment, but any mix of stone fruits will do.

Makes 18 crostini
Hands-on time: 12 minutes
Total time: 32 minutes

1 baguette

4 tablespoons extra-virgin olive oil

2 cups chopped stone fruits (such as peaches, plums, nectarines, cherries—use a mix of whatever you have on hand)

1 tablespoon chopped shallot

2 tablespoons apple cider vinegar

2 teaspoons chopped fresh thyme, plus thyme leaves for garnish

½ teaspoon kosher salt

½ teaspoon freshly ground black pepper

8 ounces burrata cheese, at room temperature

Flaky sea salt

1. Preheat the oven to 425°F.

2. Slice the baguette crosswise into ½-inch-thick slices. Place the baguette slices in a single layer on a baking sheet. Drizzle with 2 tablespoons of the olive oil. Bake for 10 minutes, or until toasted, flipping the baguette slices after 5 minutes.

3. Combine the stone fruits, shallot, vinegar, remaining 2 tablespoons olive oil, the thyme, kosher salt, and pepper in a medium bowl. Let stand for 10 minutes.

4. Smear the burrata on the baguette slices. Top with the fruit mixture. Drizzle with additional olive oil and sprinkle with the thyme leaves and salt.

Peach-Jalapeño Cornbread
with Honey Butter

Cast-iron skillets are for lovers—shouldn't that be a T-shirt? Jessica loves any opportunity to cook with ours, broken in from years of preparing meals for our children. She will be the first to tell you that she sees cornbread mostly as a vehicle for eating honey butter, but with this recipe, the sweet-and-spicy buttermilk-based bread can stand on its own. If you like extra heat, leave the seeds in the jalapeño.

Serves 8 to 12
Hands-on time: 10 minutes
Total time: 25 minutes

3 tablespoons salted butter

1 cup chopped peaches (about 1 medium)

2 jalapeños, seeded and chopped (about ⅓ cup)

1½ cups stone-ground yellow cornmeal

¼ cup all-purpose flour

1 teaspoon baking powder

1 teaspoon baking soda

1 teaspoon kosher salt

1¾ cups buttermilk

2 large eggs

HONEY BUTTER
½ cup (1 stick) salted butter, at room temperature

2 tablespoons honey

1. Preheat the oven to 450°F.

2. Melt 1 tablespoon of the butter in a 10-inch cast-iron skillet over medium-high heat; add the peaches and cook for 3 minutes, or until beginning to caramelize. Add the jalapeños; cook, stirring, for 1 minute. Transfer the peach mixture to a bowl. Place the empty skillet in the oven.

3. Whisk together the cornmeal, flour, baking powder, baking soda, and salt in a large bowl. Whisk together the buttermilk and eggs in a small bowl. Add the buttermilk mixture to the cornmeal mixture and stir until just combined. Stir in the peach mixture.

4. Carefully remove the hot skillet from the oven. Add the remaining 2 tablespoons butter and swirl the skillet to melt the butter. Pour the batter into the skillet and return it to the oven. Bake for 18 to 20 minutes, until the cornbread is golden brown. Let cool slightly before serving.

5. Meanwhile, to make the honey butter, stir together the butter and honey until smooth.

6. Serve the cornbread with the honey butter.

Sweet and Spicy Empanadas

This is one of the first recipes we developed, and we hold it dear! Warm or cool, these baked hand pies balance the salty spice of fresh sausage with the sweetness of fresh Georgia peaches, and best of all, they're ideal for breakfast, lunch, or even dinner, and easy to take on the go. The turmeric adds a lovely yellow color to the dough, which, like the filling, can be made a day ahead and kept refrigerated. Use the leftover filling in quesadillas, tacos, or lettuce cups. We've made a simple dough from scratch, but you could also make these with premade pie crust.

Makes 12 to 14 empanadas
Hands-on time: 30 minutes
Total time: 2 hours 10 minutes

DOUGH

1¾ cups all-purpose flour

½ cup fine white cornmeal

1 teaspoon kosher salt

½ teaspoon ground turmeric

½ cup (1 stick) cold unsalted butter, cut into ½-inch cubes

1 large egg

⅓ cup ice water

1 tablespoon distilled white vinegar

1. To make the dough, sift together the flour, cornmeal, salt, and turmeric into a large bowl and blend in the butter with your fingers, a fork, or a pastry cutter until the butter has been broken down into pea-size bits.

2. In a separate bowl, whisk together the egg, ice water, and vinegar. Add the wet mixture to the dry mixture and mix with a fork until just incorporated. It will still be clumpy and crumbly. Do not overmix.

3. Turn the mixture out onto a floured work surface and work the dough with the heel of your hand until it comes together in a ball. Wrap in plastic wrap and refrigerate for at least 1 hour and up to 24 hours.

FILLING

2 tablespoons olive oil

1 large onion, finely diced

1 teaspoon kosher salt

1 teaspoon smoked paprika

1 teaspoon red pepper flakes

½ teaspoon ground cumin

½ teaspoon chili powder

¼ teaspoon ground
cinnamon

2 garlic cloves, minced

½ red bell pepper, minced

1 pound sausage

3 medium peaches, pitted
and diced (about 3 cups)

2 tablespoons sugar

Heavy cream or beaten egg,
for brushing (optional)

4. To make the filling, heat the olive oil in a large skillet over medium-high heat. Add the onion and cook, stirring, until translucent. Add the salt, paprika, red pepper flakes, cumin, chili powder, cinnamon, garlic, bell pepper, and sausage and cook, breaking up the meat with a wooden spoon as it cooks, until the sausage is browned, about 8 minutes. Add the peaches and sugar, stir, and cook until the peaches are heated through, about 2 minutes. Remove from the heat. Chill the filling for 1 hour and up to 48 hours.

5. Preheat the oven to 350°F. Line a baking sheet with parchment paper.

6. Roll out your dough to ⅛-inch thickness and cut it into 4-inch circles, using a small plate or bowl as a guide. Using your fingers or a brush, wet the edge of one dough circle with water and place a mound of the filling in the center. Fold the dough over to seal the empanada, pressing along the edges to ensure a good seal. Place on the prepared baking sheet. Repeat with the remaining dough and filling. If desired, brush the empanadas with cream or egg before baking for a glossy finish. Cut a slit in each empanada to allow steam to escape while baking. Bake the empanadas on the center rack for 40 minutes, or until golden brown. Cool on a wire rack for 15 minutes before serving.

Golden Gazpacho

A refreshing puree with a clean finish, this recipe is lovely on its own or as a complement to a meal. It has also been an excellent outlet for Jessica's obsession with making soup, which charges full steam ahead in the winter, but comes to a natural halt once the hotter months begin. Refrigerating the gazpacho really brings out the balance of the flavors. You can substitute another subtle, low-acidity vinegar for the champagne vinegar, and keep the peels on the peaches for more depth. This can be served immediately, or chilled up to 24 hours before serving.

Serves 8
Hands-on time: 15 minutes
Total time: 15 minutes

6 medium peaches, peeled (see page 245), pitted, and diced

1 large English cucumber, peeled and diced

3 tablespoons champagne vinegar

¼ cup extra-virgin olive oil

1½ teaspoons sea salt

2 tablespoons chopped fresh cilantro leaves, plus whole leaves for garnish

1. Reserve ¼ cup each of the peaches and cucumber for the garnish. Place the remaining peaches and cucumber in a blender and add the vinegar, olive oil, salt, and 1 cup water. Blend on high until smooth.

2. Once smooth, stir in the cilantro and pour into serving dishes.

3. Garnish with a little of the reserved peaches and cucumber and top each with a cilantro leaf before serving.

The Marché Peach Tartine

The Marché tartine! Every summer, we hear about the dishes that chefs around town are creating with our peaches, and it never stops feeling surreal. We try to find moments between work and our babies to run out and taste whatever they've cooked up, and one that's always on our mind is the tartine at Marché Artisan Foods. The casual sister eatery to Margot Café, Marché is part of the East Nashville neighborhood that came alive more than fifteen years ago when Margot McCormack, queen chef of all chefs, decided to open her eponymous French Italian spot in what was then a boarded-up service station. The depth and beauty of this simple tartine is a perfect example of Margot's skill for making delicious, uncomplicated food. She never skimps on the peaches, creating a gorgeous mound of juicy slices under a drizzle of honey. We're grateful to her for opening her door to us, and for loving Nashville and believing in what it can be. Anyone in town will tell you that her restaurants create community, and that's because they're conceived with a lot of soul.

Because there are so few ingredients in this recipe, quality is important—so try to use the best bread, honey, and ricotta possible. Don't be shy about using a huge mound of the fruit! When we make it, we use a whole peach for each slice of bread. We enjoy this as a snack, but spend any summer day at Marché and you'll see these delivered to table after table from morning to late afternoon.

Serves 4
Hands-on time: 5 minutes
Total time: 5 minutes

1 cup whole-milk ricotta

2 tablespoons powdered sugar

1 teaspoon pure vanilla extract

4 slices good artisan bread, toasted

4 peaches, pitted and sliced

Honey, for drizzling

Stir together the ricotta, powdered sugar, and vanilla. Slather the bread generously with the mixture. Top each slice of bread with 1 whole sliced peach. Drizzle with honey. Serve immediately.

PROPER PEACH CARE

Heading home with a bag or box of juicy peaches? Here's what to do before you take a bite.

STEP 1: If your peaches are still firm, don't refrigerate them. They like the heat, so leave them out on the counter. For faster conditioning, keep them in a brown paper bag.

STEP 2: Check them daily. Are they softening? Are they fragrant? They're coming along.

STEP 3: Squeeze them. When they're ready to eat, they'll give a little, like an avocado.

STEP 4: Soft and ready to eat? Grab some napkins, take a bite, and enjoy!

STEP 5: Once they are good and soft, they'll keep wonderfully in the refrigerator for about a week.

LUNCH

MUSIC CITY LOVE SONG

We owe so much to Nashville. Not only is it where we've laid down roots—created a home, had three children, and made lasting friends and memories—but we truly believe that starting our business anywhere else would have been twice as difficult. Nashville has a long history as a city that's willing to take a bet on someone with a dream, and we count ourselves fortunate to have experienced that openness from the minute we first parked The Peach Truck at Imogene + Willie.

When we moved to the city in 2010, it was the seventh-fastest-growing metropolis in the country. Among those arriving in town were tech companies, food trucks, restaurateurs, fashion stylists, and entrepreneurs, inspired by the same kind of ambition that had for decades attracted country music artists to Music City. The energy of transplants, immigrants, and entertainers was palpable, but just before we arrived, it was stymied by a May flood that brought the city to its knees, with devastating loss of life and more than ten thousand homes damaged or destroyed. What we witnessed in those early months was the spirit of the Volunteer State—so named in 1840, when Tennesseans volunteered to fight in the Mexican-American War—alive and well in the twenty-first century in the form of people pitching in to take care of their own and put the city back together.

We could tell that there was something special about the place. Everywhere we went, it was clear there was so much bubbling up in Nashville. We remember being at a party one night, where a guy with a bit of a put-on persona told us, "Nashville is for dreamers. Whatever your dream is, do it. It can happen here." It sounded cheesy, but for whatever reason, it stuck in our minds. This is a tight-knit community of people starting things they're passionate about and just going for it. When we headed full speed into creating The Peach Truck, that same community let us set up in their parking lots and at their events, raved about us to their friends, and encouraged us to keep going.

One of the first things we knew we needed to do was to get our peaches into the hands of local chefs. Today, Nashville receives resounding accolades as a food destination, but the year we started The Peach Truck, the movement of chef-owned restaurants was only just beginning. We set out to get on chefs' radars with a set of tools that showed just how little we knew about how to sell produce: we had a website, a clipboard full of order forms, and a stack of business cards to prove we were legit.

Our first stop that summer was City House. Chef and owner Tandy Wilson, who has since earned a James Beard Award for Best Chef, Southeast, is largely credited with jump-starting the culture of chef-owned restaurants in Nashville. His Southern-inspired Italian eatery, tucked into a leafy brick house in Germantown, became a fast favorite when we moved to town. We'd see Tandy weekly at the farmers' market buying his produce, and couldn't help noticing that the wild popularity of his ingredient-led menu seemed to give other chefs the confidence that they could do something similar.

The day we pulled up to sell him peaches, it was Jessica who was bold enough to get out of the car, go around to the back door, and give it a few brave knocks. Clutching order forms and those useless business cards, she was surprised when Tandy himself answered the door. "What's up?" he said. Jessica stammered through her response while showing him an order form. "I've got peaches. They're from Georgia. We're going to get them right off the tree and bring them up and into your hands." He looked back at her. "That sounds great. Just bring the boxes and we'll go from there." In true chef fashion, he did not need a form—he just needed to see and smell the produce.

Once Tandy tasted our peaches, he, in his native Nashville way, told other chefs about us. We set up a wholesale route, appearing at back doors every week to show chefs what we'd trucked up from Georgia. Tandy told people like Tyler Brown, who was then at the Hermitage Hotel, and Margot McCormack, under whom Tandy had worked at Marché; Burger Up suddenly had a Peach Truck Old-Fashioned on the menu. We were overwhelmed by Tandy's generosity of spirit. As a small business owner, he could have kept a competitive advantage, but the attitude between chefs coming up in the city at the time was, "If you win, we all win." We were beneficiaries of that outlook, too. We had a great product, and certainly great timing, but the game changer was the place and the people cheering us on.

Today, Nashville is as exciting a place as ever, a place where you can not only hear the best music, but, thanks to the city's celebrated and up-and-coming chefs, sample some of the best food in the world, whether in established neighborhoods or out-of-the-way holes-in-the-wall. You really can have just about anything you want for lunch, and we hope this selection of recipes—from authentic tamales to hearty sandwiches and light, summery salads—gives you a taste of the breadth of midday dining in Nashville. It feels amazing every time we see our peaches in that creative, dream-worthy mix.

Prosciutto, Burrata, and Pan-Roasted Peach Salad

We love how the textures in this salad—the crispy prosciutto, smooth burrata, pulpy peaches, and stalky arugula—play off one another. A peppery arugula is our favorite for this dish, but feel free to substitute baby spinach or mixed greens. The dressing can be made ahead, and once the components of the salad have been cooked, it's easy to take on the go and assemble. Salty, creamy, juicy, and sharp? Yes, please!

Makes 8 cups; serves 4
Hands-on time: 15 minutes
Total time: 15 minutes

¼ cup white balsamic vinegar

1 tablespoon Dijon mustard

½ teaspoon kosher salt

½ teaspoon freshly ground black pepper

1 tablespoon chopped fresh chives

⅓ cup plus 1 tablespoon extra-virgin olive oil

4 ounces thinly sliced prosciutto

2 medium peaches, pitted and quartered

5 ounces arugula

½ pound burrata cheese

1. Whisk together the vinegar, mustard, salt, pepper, and chives in a small bowl. While whisking, slowly drizzle in the ⅓ cup olive oil and whisk until the dressing is emulsified.

2. Working in batches, cook the prosciutto in a large skillet over medium-high heat, turning occasionally, for 2 to 3 minutes, until crispy. Transfer the prosciutto to a plate. Add the 1 tablespoon olive oil to the skillet. Working in batches, add the peaches and cook for 1 to 2 minutes per side, until browned. Remove from the heat.

3. Toss the arugula with ¼ cup of the dressing in a medium bowl. Divide the arugula among four plates. Top evenly with the prosciutto and peaches. Tear the burrata into 1-inch pieces and divide it among the salads. Serve with additional dressing on the side.

Freekeh Peach Power Bowl

This healthy bowl of nutrition-packed foods will make you feel like your best self. The recipe was actually a slow discovery over time—Jessica realized she was taking our leftovers and throwing them in a bowl with a flavorful dressing. Now it's a go-to in our family—often with an over-medium egg on top.

Use any grain you like—quinoa, farro, rice, bulgur, and buckwheat all work—just adjust the water and cooking time according to the package directions. The chickpeas can be swapped out for lentils or other beans. You'll want to massage the heck out of the raw kale so that it really softens. This is a great meal-prep dish: cook the grain ahead and assemble your lunches for the week—just slice the peach before eating!

Serves 4
Hands-on time: 30 minutes
Total time: 30 minutes

1½ cups cracked freekeh

2 teaspoons kosher salt

½ cup extra-virgin olive oil

¼ cup fresh lemon juice

½ teaspoon freshly ground
   black pepper

1 tablespoon honey

1 garlic clove, minced

2 teaspoons chopped
   fresh oregano

4 cups thinly sliced lacinato
   (Tuscan or dinosaur) kale
   (4 ounces)

½ cup thinly sliced red onion

1 large peach, pitted and
   thinly sliced

1 cup cooked chickpeas

4 ounces feta cheese,
   crumbled

½ cup sunflower seeds,
   toasted

1. Combine the freekeh, 3 cups water, and 1 teaspoon of the salt in a medium saucepan. Bring to a boil over medium-high heat. Reduce the heat to medium-low, cover, and cook until the freekeh is tender, about 25 minutes. Drain.

2. Whisk together the olive oil, lemon juice, remaining 1 teaspoon salt, the pepper, honey, garlic, and oregano in a small bowl. Toss the kale with 2 tablespoons of the dressing in a large bowl. Using your hands, massage the kale until it darkens and begins to soften.

3. Divide the freekeh, kale, onion, peach, chickpeas, feta, and sunflower seeds among four bowls. Serve with the remaining dressing.

Cobb Salad

with Peach Candied Bacon

With fresh ingredients that don't require an oven, a Cobb salad in the summer is always a welcome idea. This is a classic, satisfying version with a subtle twist that will likely catch off guard friends or family to whom you serve it. *What, exactly, makes it so good?* they will wonder. The answer is two tablespoons of our Signature Peach Jam, which gives the salad a tangy kick that picks up the peachy notes of the bacon. You can make the dressing and cook the eggs up to two days before serving.

Serves 4; makes ½ cup dressing

Hands-on time: 10 minutes

Total time: 10 minutes

DRESSING

2 tablespoons
   red wine vinegar

2 tablespoons fresh
   lemon juice

1 tablespoon stone-ground
   mustard

2 tablespoons The Peach
   Truck Signature Peach Jam
   (page 263)

¾ teaspoon kosher salt

½ teaspoon freshly ground
   black pepper

⅓ cup extra-virgin olive oil

SALAD

1 (1 pound) head romaine
   lettuce, chopped (7 cups)

4 slices Peach Candied
   Bacon (page 37), crumbled

1 cup chopped cooked
   chicken

2 hard-boiled eggs, peeled
   and sliced

1 cup halved grape tomatoes

½ cup chopped red onion

1 avocado, diced

4 ounces blue cheese,
   crumbled (1 cup)

1. To make the dressing, whisk together the vinegar, lemon juice, mustard, jam, salt, and pepper in a small bowl. While whisking, slowly drizzling in the olive oil and whisk until the dressing is emulsified.

2. To make the salad, arrange the lettuce on a platter and top with the bacon, chicken, eggs, tomatoes, onion, avocado, and cheese. Serve with the dressing alongside.

Fresh Herb Omelet

with Peach Bruschetta

Sometimes an omelet for lunch can feel dainty, but the bruschetta here, with its generous heaping of tender onions and peaches, gives it just enough oomph. Use your favorite cheese—Taleggio, robiola, goat cheese, ricotta, burrata—and for herbs, sprinkle in whatever you have on hand. A mix of fresh mint, chives, parsley, thyme, oregano, and tarragon would balance nicely with the other ingredients. We suggest letting the eggs stand for fifteen minutes once they've been beaten for a softer, creamier omelet. You can make the caramelized onions up to one week ahead.

Serves 4
Hands-on time: 45 minutes
Total time: 1 hour

2 tablespoons olive oil

1 large sweet onion, cut into ¼-inch-thick slices (about 3 cups)

1 medium peach, pitted and thinly sliced (about 1 cup)

1 teaspoon kosher salt

¼ teaspoon freshly ground black pepper

8 large eggs

3 tablespoons chopped mixed fresh herbs

2 tablespoons salted butter

8 slices baguette, toasted

4 ounces softened cheese, such as Gorgonzola, Camembert, or Taleggio

1. Heat the olive oil in a large skillet over medium heat. Add the onion and cook, stirring occasionally, for 20 minutes, then continue to cook, stirring frequently, for 10 minutes more, or until golden brown. Add the peach, ½ teaspoon of the salt, and the pepper. Cook for 5 minutes, or until the peach is softened.

2. Whisk together the eggs, herbs, 2 tablespoons water, and remaining ½ teaspoon salt in a medium bowl until smooth. Let stand for 15 minutes.

3. Melt 1 tablespoon of the butter in a 10-inch pan over medium heat. Add half the egg mixture (about 1 cup) and cook for 1 minute, or until the sides are set. Using a wooden spoon, drag the cooked sides into the middle of the pan, letting the uncooked eggs run out and underneath. Repeat until the top is set but still moist. Remove the omelet from the pan; fold it in half. Repeat the process with the remaining 1 tablespoon butter and egg mixture. Cut each omelet in half.

4. Place one omelet half on each of four plates. Top the baguette slices evenly with the cheese. Spoon about 2 heaping tablespoons of the onion mixture onto each baguette slice and serve them alongside the omelets.

Edley's Sweet Georgia Brown

Doesn't the sight of those peach rounds lined up underneath pulled pork dripping with barbecue sauce make you want to close this cookbook immediately and drive to your local barbecue spot? Stephen, who considers barbecue pulled pork a way of life, can relate to that feeling. The sandwich that's usually on his mind is this one, from the Nashville institution Edley's Bar-B-Que, where they combine smoky pork with fresh, cold peaches and create an outright dream. We love this sandwich. We wait in line for this sandwich. People visiting from out of town inquire about when we'll be going to eat this sandwich.

One way to prepare this is by using pulled pork from your favorite BBQ joint (our condolences if it's not Edley's). Or you can make your own distinctively smoky version from the recipe that follows. If you do, a digital probe thermometer is the easiest way to monitor the temperature of the meat. Either way, dress it with our Peach Bourbon BBQ Sauce or your favorite store-bought sauce and dig in!

Serves 12

Hands-on time: 8 hours 15 minutes

Total time: 9 hours 45 minutes, plus overnight

PORK

¼ cup paprika

2 tablespoons kosher salt

¼ cup packed dark brown
  sugar

1½ teaspoons dry mustard

1 tablespoon garlic powder

2 tablespoon freshly ground
  black pepper

1 teaspoon cayenne pepper

1 (6-to-8 pound) bone-in
  pork shoulder (also known
  as a Boston butt)

¼ cup peanut oil

⅓ cup apple cider vinegar

⅓ cup peach nectar
  or apple juice

8 cups wood chunks of
  your choice

TO ASSEMBLE

12 hamburger buns, toasted

2¼ cup Peach Bourbon BBQ
  Sauce (page 255) or your
  favorite red BBQ sauce

¾ cup thin peach slices
  (about 12 ounces)

3½ pounds chopped
  cooked pork, warmed

24 dill pickle chips

1. Combine the paprika, salt, brown sugar, mustard, garlic powder, black pepper, and cayenne in a medium bowl. Trim the fat on the pork to ¼-inch thickness. Rub the pork all over with peanut oil. Sprinkle the paprika mixture all over the pork, coating completely. Chill, uncovered, overnight.

2. Combine the vinegar and nectar in a food-safe spray bottle. Soak the wood chunks in water for at least 30 minutes. Let the pork stand at room temperature for 30 minutes.

3. Prepare the smoker with a water pan and heat to 250°F to 275°F. Place pork, fat side up, in the smoker. Cover and smoke for 4 to 6 hours, spritzing with the vinegar mixture every hour, until the temperature in the thickest portion of the pork reads 165°F (make sure the thermometer is not touching the bone). Place the pork in a foil pan and cover tightly with foil. If you don't have a foil pan, you can wrap the pork tightly in a double layer of foil. Place the wrapped pork back on the smoker, cover, and cook for 2 to 4 more hours, or until the temperature in the thickest portion of the pork reads 200°F, the heat at which the collagen in the meat breaks down and the meat achieves its texture.

4. Remove the pork from the smoker. Let it rest, wrapped in foil, for 1 to 2 hours before pulling the meat.

5. To make the sandwiches, spread the bottom of each bun with 1 tablespoon of the BBQ sauce. Top evenly with the peach slices and pork. Drizzle with the remaining sauce and top with the pickle slices. Set the top halves of the buns over the pickles and serve immediately.

Summer Garden Pasta

Served warm or cold, this pasta with fresh corn, basil, tomato, and sweet peach brings the bounty of the season to your table. We make it all the time at home because it's so easy and enjoyable, and it's also great for packing up to bring to work. If you're looking to add some protein, try shredded cooked chicken breast or a few grilled shrimp.

Makes 8 cups
Hands-on time: 20 minutes
Total time: 20 minutes

12 ounces casarecce pasta

1 tablespoon lemon zest

2 tablespoons fresh lemon juice

2 tablespoons balsamic vinegar

1 tablespoon minced shallot

1 garlic clove, minced

1 teaspoon kosher salt

½ teaspoon freshly ground black pepper

⅓ cup extra-virgin olive oil

2 tablespoons chopped fresh basil, plus basil leaves for garnish

¼ cup pine nuts, toasted

1½ cups multicolored cherry tomatoes, halved

1 cup chopped peaches (about 1 medium)

1 cup fresh corn kernels

Freshly grated Parmesan cheese

1. Bring a large pot of salted water to a boil. Add the pasta; cook according to the package directions. Drain.

2. Whisk together the lemon zest, lemon juice, vinegar, shallot, garlic, salt, and pepper in a large bowl. While whisking, slowly drizzle in the olive oil and whisk until emulsified. Add the pasta, chopped basil, pine nuts, tomatoes, peaches, and corn and toss well.

3. Serve the pasta with a sprinkling of the basil leaves and Parmesan.

The Peach Truck BLP

Is there anything more summery than a BLT? There is indeed! Made with succulent peaches instead of tomatoes, and slathered with a sweet-and-spicy honey-pepper mayo, this sandwich literally drips with the flavors of summer. We recommend taking it to the next level by using our Peach Candied Bacon (page 37).

Serves 4
Hands-on time: 10 minutes
Total time: 10 minutes

4 tablespoons Duke's mayonnaise

1 tablespoon wildflower honey

1 teaspoon freshly ground black pepper

8 slices bread, toasted

12 to 16 slices bacon, cooked until crispy

4 or 5 medium peaches, pitted and sliced ¼ inch thick

4 to 8 Bibb lettuce leaves

1. Stir together the mayonnaise, honey, and pepper in a small bowl and spread the mixture on one side of each slice of bread.

2. Arrange the peach slices evenly over half the slices of bread.

3. On the remaining slices of bread, arrange the bacon slices and lettuce leaves, dividing them evenly.

4. Place the bacon-lettuce bread slices on top of the slices with the peach to form sandwiches and enjoy.

Fried Catfish

with Fresh Peach Salsa

Catfish in the South can sometimes be code for heavily breaded, low-quality fish, but we've watched this recipe win people over because of its light dusting of cornmeal which becomes even more delectably salty when paired with the fresh peach salsa. The fried catfish is also a great base for other meals—serve it with a salad and Peach-Jalapeño Cornbread (page 80), or in tacos alongside sriracha mayo, shredded purple cabbage, and diced peach and avocado.

Serves 8
Hands-on time: 30 minutes
Total time: 30 minutes

PEACH SALSA

3 medium peaches, peeled
   (see page 245), pitted, and
   diced (about 3 cups)

2 green onions, chopped

¾ cup diced jicama

¼ cup diced cucumber

¼ teaspoon ground coriander

¼ cup chopped fresh cilantro

1 small jalapeño,
   seeded and diced

½ teaspoon kosher salt

Pinch of freshly grated
   nutmeg

CATFISH

Vegetable oil, for frying

2 cups fine yellow cornmeal

1 tablespoon kosher salt

2 teaspoons freshly ground
   black pepper

¼ teaspoon cayenne pepper

½ teaspoon garlic powder

2 cups buttermilk

8 (6-ounce) catfish fillets

1 lemon, cut into wedges,
   for serving

1. To make the salsa, combine the peaches, green onions, jicama, cucumber, coriander, cilantro, jalapeño, ½ teaspoon salt, and the nutmeg in a medium bowl.

2. To fry the catfish, fill a large, heavy, deep skillet with vegetable oil to a depth of 1½ inches. Heat the oil over medium-high heat to 350°F. Line a plate with paper towels and set it nearby.

3. Whisk together the cornmeal, 1 tablespoon salt, the black pepper, cayenne, and garlic powder in a shallow dish. Pour the buttermilk into a second shallow dish. Coat the catfish fillets one at a time in the buttermilk, then dip them into the cornmeal mixture, coating them completely. Shake off the excess cornmeal. Working in batches, fry the fillets in the oil until golden brown, about 3 minutes per side. Drain on the paper towels. Season with salt.

4. Serve the catfish with the lemon wedges and peach salsa.

Savory Cornmeal Crepes

This is a great use for your summer veggies—especially if you joined a CSA and keep wondering what you're going to do with all that zucchini. This crepe is light, and can be as healthy as you'd like, depending on how seriously you pack in the vegetables.

To cook, add batter to the skillet by pouring it into the center, then tilt the skillet so its entire surface is covered. Be sure to re-stir the batter and redistribute the cornmeal before making each new crepe. Prior to adding the ricotta, warm it in a small saucepan over medium heat or in the microwave for thirty seconds, stirring occasionally, so that it spreads effortlessly onto the crepe.

Serves 4
Hands-on time: 25 minutes
Total time: 25 minutes

2 tablespoons olive oil

1 cup diced peaches
(about 1 medium)

1 cup diced summer squash

1 teaspoon kosher salt

½ teaspoon freshly ground
black pepper

5 ounces baby spinach

1 large egg

¾ cup whole milk

¼ cup all-purpose flour

¼ cup fine cornmeal

Unsalted butter, for greasing

1 cup ricotta cheese,
warmed (see headnote)

8 tablespoons Savory Peach
Butter (page 256), melted

¼ cup chopped fresh parsley

1. Heat the olive oil in a large skillet over medium-high heat. Add the peaches, squash, ½ teaspoon of the salt, and the pepper and cook, stirring occasionally, for 3 to 4 minutes, until tender. Add the spinach and stir until it begins to wilt. Remove from the heat.

2. Whisk together the egg, milk, flour, cornmeal, and remaining ½ teaspoon salt in a medium bowl.

3. Heat a 10-inch nonstick skillet over medium heat. Brush the surface of the skillet lightly with butter. Add ¼ of the batter (about 5 tablespoons) to the center of the skillet and cook for 2 minutes, or until the edges of the crepe begin to brown. Loosen crepe with a spatula and flip; cook for 30 seconds, or until dry and set. Transfer to a plate. Repeat with the remaining batter, placing a piece of parchment or waxed paper between each crepe on the plate.

4. Divide the crepes among individual plates. Spread ¼ cup of the ricotta onto each crepe. Spoon about ½ cup of the peach mixture on top. Fold the crepes in half over the filling. Serve the crepes drizzled with melted peach butter and sprinkled with parsley.

The Grilled Cheeserie's Shaved Peach Melt

The Grilled Cheeserie started as a food truck shortly before we did, and we've collaborated as we've come up together. Husband-and-wife team Joseph Bogan and Crystal De Luna-Bogan take a gourmet approach to the simple melted-cheese staple, and the results are mouthwatering combinations made with locally sourced, seasonal ingredients. They take the same care with soups, tater tots, and milk shakes—into which our peaches are blended every summer.

This melt is incredible with Buttercup cheese, a small-batch variety made in North Carolina, which we get from the Bloomy Rind in Nashville. If you can't find Buttercup, use Muenster, or another cheese that melts easily.

Makes 1 sandwich
Hands-on time: 10 minutes
Total time: 10 minutes

2 teaspoons pickled mustard seeds or whole-grain mustard

1 teaspoon honey

3 slices English Farmstead Buttercup Cheese (2½ ounces)

½ small peach, pitted and very thinly sliced (about ⅓ cup)

4 or 5 fresh basil leaves, torn

2 (½-inch-thick) slices bakery-style bread

1 tablespoon salted butter

1. Combine the mustard seeds and honey in a small bowl. Arrange the cheese slices, peach slices, and basil on one slice of the bread. Drizzle with the mustard mixture. Top with the remaining bread slice.

2. Melt the butter in a medium skillet over medium heat. Add the sandwich; cook for 2 minutes on each side, or until the bread is golden and toasted and the cheese has melted. Serve immediately.

Mas Tacos Peach Tamales

Tamales are a labor of love. Requiring some time and lots of careful folding, they always blow us away at Mas Tacos Por Favor, where owner Teresa Mason whips them up effortlessly. Her soulful spin on Mexican cuisine has been a vital part of our lives, and we're not the only ones who feel this way. A much-loved lunch spot with a chalkboard menu and a line out the door, Mas Tacos features our peaches in a special tamale on Wednesdays throughout the summer. We're honored to be a small part of this incredible Nashville institution.

Makes about 40 tamales
Hands-on time: 50 minutes
Total time: 1 hour 30 minutes

1 bag corn husks (available in a Mexican market, the international aisle of the grocery store, or online)

6 cups masa harina (a traditional Mexican corn flour used for tamales)

2 teaspoons kosher salt, plus more as needed

2 teaspoons baking powder

1 cup solid coconut oil

6 cups sweet corn broth or any clear broth you like, at room temperature

12 medium peaches, pitted and sliced

18 ounces queso fresco, crumbled

½ cup honey

¼ teaspoon red pepper flakes

Pinch of kosher salt

1. Soak the corn husks in warm water until soft, about 1 hour.

2. Whisk together the masa harina, salt, and baking powder in a large bowl.

3. Using a handheld mixer, whip the coconut oil until light and creamy. Add the broth and whipped coconut oil to the masa mixture and beat with the mixer or stir by hand until smooth. Cover and chill while you prepare the peaches. The mixture will be ready to use right away.

4. Spread about 3 tablespoons of the masa mixture evenly over each corn husk in a loose rectangle shape (around 5 x 3 inches or so). Lay a few peach slices and about 2 tablespoons of the queso fresco on top of the masa.

5. Fold the sides of the corn husk to the center so that they overlap over the masa. Fold the empty part of the husk under so that it rests against the side of the tamale with a seam. Tie with butcher twine, but not too tightly. You don't want to make a "waistline" when they steam.

6. Pour about 1 cup water into the bottom of a tamale steamer, large Dutch oven, or stockpot fitted with a steamer basket and place the tamales in the basket and cover the pot. Bring the water to a boil over medium-high heat. Reduce the heat to medium-low. Cook the tamales for 35 to 40 minutes, checking them for doneness after 20 minutes and adding more water as needed.

THE PEACH TRUCK COOKBOOK

The tamales are cooked when the masa mixture separates easily from the corn husk.

7.   Stir together the honey, red pepper flakes, and salt in a small bowl. Serve with the tamales.

NASHVILLE FOOD GUIDE

Nashville's culinary landscape is changing daily, with more food and drink options than we can keep up with. Here are a few of our favorite spots.

ARNOLD'S COUNTRY KITCHEN

"Meat & 3"—a meat and three sides, served up cafeteria-style—is a Nashville staple, and nobody does it better than Arnold's. We bring every visitor here because you must go with a group—you definitely want to taste as many sides as possible. Don't even try to pick. Hunker down with your pork chop, brisket, or fried shrimp and sample mac 'n' cheese, collard greens, fried green tomatoes, and creamed corn. And don't leave without a slice of chess, chocolate cream, or strawberry pie.

URBAN COWBOY'S PUBLIC HOUSE

Attached to a charming bed-and-breakfast, East Nashville's Public House has an ideal atmosphere with the drinks to match. Enjoy a Penicillin (blended Scotch whiskey, lemon juice, honey-ginger syrup, and single-malt Scotch) or another artisanal cocktail from their excellent drinks program. With a courtyard full of open fire pits and restored furniture, this is a year-round watering hole that is surprisingly unpretentious. Bring your kids, bring your dogs.

CITY HOUSE

One of the establishments in the Nashville food scene that started it all, Tandy Wilson's City House is a Southern take on Italian food, and it's absolutely perfect. Make sure you get the belly ham pizza with an egg on it (or any of their pizzas with homemade mayonnaise, really), and try their half chicken with seasonal vegetables. Do not, under any circumstances, forget to save room for dessert; Tandy has the best pastry chef in town, Rebecca Turshen, who makes a mean Tennessee Waltz Cake.

PRINCE'S HOT CHICKEN SHACK

Hot chicken is a pride and joy of Nashville, and Prince's—with its secret cayenne-heavy spice blend—is to thank for that. They've been making hot chicken for more than seventy years, with a menu so notorious, some options come with a warning. Don't go before midnight, and don't order any hotter than medium, unless you're a glutton for punishment.

MARTIN'S BAR-B-QUE JOINT

Serving West Tennessee–style whole-hog BBQ, our favorite Martin's location is the sprawling space downtown, where there are over thirty types of beers and a Ping-Pong table we know well. Owner Pat Martin lovingly refers to his eateries as "temples of smoked meats," and once you try the whole hog with a little slaw on the side or the redneck taco (a choice of pork, brisket, sausage, chicken, turkey, or catfish on a cornbread hoecake), you'll see what he means.

HENRIETTA RED

Henrietta Red's oyster bar does it up right, but everything on the larger menu is as beautiful as the space in which it's served. None of the ambiance or interiors come at the expense of their food and cocktails, however, which talk the talk. In addition to red snapper crudo and linguine clam pasta, there's plenty on offer if seafood isn't your thing. You won't leave hungry—especially if you get the vegan peach cobbler with lavender sherbet for dessert.

CAFE ROZE

An all-day café in East Nashville, Cafe Roze is the brainchild of Julia Jaksic, executive chef at Employees Only Singapore and former chef at Jack's Wife Freda in New York. Hers is a substantive, healthy, approachable menu that makes you feel good about what you're eating. Jessica always gets the egg bowl with a poached egg, kale, and preserved lemon yogurt. Stephen loves the stout waffles with poached peaches in the summer. We both go crazy for the seared half of lemony tomato in the Simple Breakfast.

DOZEN BAKERY

Dozen is great for lunchtime—try their salad and sandwich combo on one of their oven-warm baguettes. You'll also likely want to take something to go—cookies, blueberry muffins, croissants, or a fresh loaf. They also make a mean pie, and we're always delighted when our peaches make it into one.

BASTION

Bastion is split into two spaces: a cocktail bar strung with café lights that serves unbelievable nachos with pulled pork and pickled onion, and a twenty-four-seat restaurant with a five-course à la carte menu. Our advice for visiting the restaurant is to embrace adventure: have them bring you everything on the tasting menu. You can thank us later.

SIDES

IT'S ALL A GIFT

Getting into the fruit-selling business meant shifting the way we thought about nature entirely. There's a certain romance associated with living off the land, but to say we have no control of our season is an understatement: Mother Nature dictates our livelihood.

It's an especially high-stakes relationship because peaches are particular, requiring a specific set of conditions to flourish: a cold, wet winter followed by a long, hot summer. They need temperatures to increase gradually in the spring, with no cold snaps or late freezes, and it's best if there isn't too much rain during the day in the summer, so tractors don't get stuck in the orchards when it comes time for picking. If trees don't have enough winter chill hours below 45°F, the harvest will be minimal and the peaches will be lacking in quality and consistency.

It's all enough to make you have a completely sleepless March.

For Stephen, that's exactly how the month of March used to be. In our earliest years, March, the month when peach trees are most susceptible to a late frost wiping out the entire crop, gave Stephen weeks of insomnia. He'd check his weather app at all hours and call frantically down to Pearson Farm every morning. So much seemed to hang in the balance: the snowballing effect of a bad harvest would mean our supply might fall short of projections; Pearson Farm itself would take a blow; and the people picking on the farm, who make their year's earnings from February to August, would be impacted.

Jessica takes the opposite approach, leaving everything—including her emotions—in nature's hands and sleeping beautifully. Her thinking is, *What is to come will come, and we'll face it when we know the facts*. And in the seven years that we have been doing this, we've never gotten answers: trees in an orchard don't work that way. Sometimes after a frost their buds will look like they're dead and then miraculously pop back to life a few days later. Other times, buds that appear healthy will suddenly take a turn for the worse. But the farm has never been in a hurry to rush the outcome, so we've learned from them. Their attitude is, "Let's get the right answer, not the quickest one."

This patience and ability to look at things holistically has shifted our larger understanding of seasons, business, and life. In 2017, for example, we lost 85 percent of our crop to a warm winter combined with a late-spring freeze. And the strange thing was, no one panicked. The farm has been dealing with nature's unpredictability for more than a century. They had advised us to save for a rainy day, and we had.

What happened was that we got out of the middle of the circle and came to the edge of it, so we could look at the bigger picture. It brought us an unprecedented sense of gratitude, humility, and appreciation for what we *did* have to sell that year. Knowing what the peaches had withstood, and how much went into growing them, made us all the more grateful. These days, arriving at peach season every year feels remarkable, like a small miracle every time we make it.

Like the soil, sunshine, cool nights, careful pruning, and discerning thinning of trees that precede picking a ripe peach, sides in a meal can be overlooked or taken for granted, but they are integral to the whole. We often feel that the sides are even better than the main course, a chance to combine a medley of different tastes and influences in one meal. In Nashville, you only have to take a look at the Meat & 3s dotting almost every corner to see that the sides are the real stars of the show.

The recipes in this section are attractions in their own right: creative, complex dishes that demonstrate a level of effort and care, not to mention offer an element of surprise. Isn't it delightful when a peach shows up in something—a fritter, say, or a platter of fried green tomatoes—when you weren't expecting it? Peaches add freshness and tang to a meal, reflect the bounty of the season, and bring color to the table. They show that you've gone that extra step. So we'd suggest not skimping on this chapter, or the recipes within it. Pile them onto your plate.

Warm Farro

with Peaches, Cherries, and Kale

A colorful and hearty summer salad, this looks beautiful plated, and the bright, lemony dressing does a nice job of connecting all the flavors and textures. Serve it warm, cold, or at room temperature; if warm, the goat cheese melts, which is divine. Black pepper will do, if you don't have Aleppo pepper on hand, and for more heat, substitute red pepper flakes.

Makes 7 cups
Hands-on time: 30 minutes
Total time: 30 minutes

1½ cups farro

1 teaspoon lemon zest

2 tablespoons fresh
　lemon juice

1 tablespoon Dijon mustard

2 teaspoons chopped
　fresh thyme

1 garlic clove, minced

½ teaspoon kosher salt,
　plus more as needed

¼ teaspoon Aleppo pepper

6 tablespoons extra-virgin
　olive oil

6 cups chopped kale leaves
　(3½ ounces)

1 medium peach, pitted and
　chopped (about 1 cup)

1 cup pitted cherries, halved

3 ounces goat cheese,
　crumbled

½ cup chopped pistachios

1. Bring 4 cups salted water to a boil in a medium saucepan. Add the farro, reduce the heat to maintain a simmer, and cook for 20 to 25 minutes, until al dente. Drain.

2. Whisk together the lemon zest, lemon juice, mustard, thyme, garlic, salt, and pepper in a small bowl. While whisking, slowly drizzle in 4 tablespoons of the olive oil and whisk until the dressing is emulsified.

3. Heat the remaining 2 tablespoons olive oil in a large skillet over medium-high heat. Add the kale and a pinch of salt; cook, stirring occasionally, for 3 minutes, or until tender. Add the farro, peach, cherries, goat cheese, and dressing and toss well. Transfer to a bowl and serve sprinkled with the pistachios.

Savory Peach Fritters

We enjoy upending expectations sometimes, like with these fritters. You might be expecting something dessertlike, but here peaches are used to bring depth and excitement to a savory side. Similar to hush puppies, these fritters are much lighter, with a soft, tender crumb. Serve them with Peach Chutney (page 258) or dip them in Peach Hot Sauce. We dare you to stop at one.

Makes 14 fritters
Hands-on time: 25 minutes
Total time: 25 minutes

1 cup mayonnaise (our favorite is Duke's)

¼ cup Peach Hot Sauce (page 271) or sriracha

4 teaspoons fresh lemon juice

1¾ teaspoons kosher salt

2 cups all-purpose flour

2 teaspoons baking powder

¾ teaspoon garlic powder

¾ teaspoon ground coriander

1 cup whole milk

1 cup finely chopped peaches (about 1 medium)

½ cup finely chopped red bell pepper

1 cup finely chopped green onions

3 ounces Monterey Jack cheese, shredded

Vegetable oil, for frying

1. Whisk together the mayonnaise, hot sauce, lemon juice, and ¼ teaspoon of the salt. Cover and set aside.

2. Whisk together the flour, baking powder, remaining 1½ teaspoons salt, the garlic powder, and the coriander in a large bowl. Add the milk, stirring just to combine. Stir in the peaches, bell pepper, green onions, and cheese.

3. Fill a large Dutch oven or deep skillet with vegetable oil to a depth of 2 inches. Heat the oil over medium heat to 325°F. Line a baking sheet with paper towels and set it nearby.

4. Working in batches, carefully drop the batter by ¼ cupfuls into the hot oil and fry the fritters, turning occasionally, for 6 minutes, or until golden brown. Drain on the paper towels. Serve warm with the sauce for dipping.

Black-Eyed Peas

with Peach Chutney

A Southern standby, black-eyed peas were one of the memorable sides at Yoder's—the cafeteria-style restaurant run by the Mennonites that Stephen's family would trek to in Montezuma, Georgia. These are especially flavorful, thanks to the onion, garlic, thyme, and bay leaves. If you'd prefer them vegetarian, use olive oil and omit the bacon, and substitute vegetable broth for the chicken stock.

Serves 6

Hands-on time: 15 minutes

Total time: 1 hour 45 minutes, plus overnight soaking (if using dried beans)

½ pound bacon, chopped

1 small onion, chopped (about 1 cup)

1 pound fresh or dried black-eyed peas, soaked overnight if dried

2 garlic cloves, smashed

2 bay leaves

3 thyme sprigs

1¼ teaspoons kosher salt

½ teaspoon freshly ground black pepper

2½ cups unsalted chicken stock

6 tablespoons Peach Chutney (page 258)

Peach Hot Sauce (page 271), to serve

1. Line a plate with paper towels and set it nearby. Cook the bacon in a large Dutch oven over medium heat until crisp. Transfer the bacon to the paper towels to drain, reserving the drippings in the pot. When cool enough to handle, crumble the bacon.

2. Add the onion to the Dutch oven and cook for 2 minutes, or until softened. Add the peas, garlic, bay leaves, thyme sprigs, salt, pepper, and stock. Cover and bring to a boil; reduce the heat to maintain a simmer and cook, covered, for 1 hour 30 minutes, or until the peas are tender. Remove and discard the garlic, bay leaves, and thyme sprigs.

3. Ladle ½ cup of the peas into each of six bowls and stir 1 tablespoon of the chutney into each. Top with a sprinkle of the crumbled bacon and serve with the hot sauce on the side.

Sweet Cucumber Basil Salad

This salad has simple ingredients, but when they are summer fresh, it is not to be passed up! The first summer that we planted a garden, we grew basil for homemade pesto and cucumbers for juicing and dipping into hummus. When our daughter, Florence, started twisting off giant cucumbers that were more than a foot long and our basil plants were starting to form more of a basil hedge, we knew we had to start getting a little more creative with our vegetables. This dish, which balances simple Greek flavors with ripe peaches, is the mouthwatering result.

Serves 6
Hands-on time: 10 minutes
Total time: 20 minutes

2 tablespoons fresh lemon juice

2 tablespoons red wine vinegar

2 teaspoons Dijon mustard

½ teaspoon kosher salt

½ teaspoon freshly ground black pepper

⅓ cup extra-virgin olive oil

6 Persian cucumbers, halved lengthwise and sliced into half-moons (about 3 cups)

2 medium peaches, pitted, cut into wedges, and sliced crosswise (about 2 cups)

¾ cup thinly sliced sweet onion

3 ounces feta cheese, crumbled (¾ cup)

½ cup torn fresh basil leaves

1. Whisk together the lemon juice, vinegar, mustard, salt, and pepper in a medium bowl. While whisking, slowly drizzle in the olive oil and whisk until emulsified. Add the cucumbers, peaches, and onion. Let stand for 10 minutes.

2. Stir in the feta and basil and serve.

Fresh Summer Asian Salad

In 2013, after we finished our second peach season, we took off on a five-month trip around the world, including six weeks in India. We zigzagged across the country, starting in Kolkata and ending in New Delhi, with a visit to Nepal along the way. One evening, on a rooftop in the northern city of Varanasi, we ate a peanut salad that we still think about to this day. Creating one for this cookbook felt special—a nod to that extraordinary trip and something that we really wanted to get right. We think we did. The Thai chile and basil, which can be found at your local Asian market; the fish sauce, which contributes complex salty flavors to the dish; the fresh fruits tumbled together with the crunch of peanuts—this is the magic you long for in a summery side dish.

Serves 6 to 8
Hands-on time: 15 minutes
Total time: 15 minutes

1 Thai chile, minced

1 garlic clove, minced

¼ cup fresh lime juice

2 tablespoons fish sauce

1 tablespoon vegetable oil

1 tablespoon light brown
   sugar

1 shallot, thinly sliced
   (about ¼ cup)

1 pound watermelon, peeled
   and cut into ¼-inch-thick
   matchsticks (about 3 cups)

1 mango, pitted, peeled, and
   cut into ¼-inch-thick
   matchsticks (about 1 cup)

2 medium peaches, pitted
   and cut into ¼-inch-thick
   matchsticks (about 2 cups)

1 cucumber, peeled, seeded,
   and cut into ¼-inch-thick
   matchsticks (about 1¼ cups)

½ cup fresh Thai basil leaves

½ cup fresh mint leaves

½ cup chopped dry-roasted
   peanuts

1. Whisk together the chile, garlic, lime juice, fish sauce, vegetable oil, brown sugar, and shallot in a large bowl. Set aside ½ cup in a separate small bowl.

2. Add the watermelon, mango, peaches, cucumber, basil, and mint to the large bowl, tossing well. Sprinkle with the peanuts and serve with the reserved dressing on the side for dipping or drizzling.

Caramelized Brussels Sprouts

It has been so nice to see Brussels sprouts make a comeback after our parents' generation spent years ruining them with steam. They're a great base for so many flavors, and this recipe uses them to full advantage in a crispy combination of spicy and sweet. If you want them hotter, go heavier on the red pepper flakes. And as a bonus, you can easily substitute green beans or broccoli.

Serves 4
Hands-on time: 10 minutes
Total time: 10 minutes

1 tablespoon vegetable oil

1 pound Brussels sprouts, trimmed and halved lengthwise

2 tablespoons unseasoned rice vinegar

3 tablespoons The Peach Truck Signature Peach Jam (page 263)

½ teaspoon fish sauce

2 teaspoons soy sauce

2 garlic cloves, minced

1 teaspoon minced fresh ginger

¼ teaspoon red pepper flakes

1. Heat the vegetable oil in a large skillet over medium-high heat. Add the Brussels sprouts and cook, turning them occasionally, until browned and just tender, about 5 minutes.

2. Whisk together the vinegar, jam, fish sauce, soy sauce, garlic, ginger, and red pepper flakes in a small bowl. Add the mixture to the Brussels sprouts in the skillet. Cook for 2 minutes, or until the liquid has thickened slightly. Serve warm.

Zucchini Stir Fry

This vegetable dish feels surprisingly decadent, thanks to the depth of the flavors—the serrano, shallots, and soy sauce—tied together with sweet Peach Chutney. If you don't have time to fry the shallots, buy them pre-fried at an Asian market, and if you'd like less heat, remove the seeds from the serrano before slicing it. Once the zucchini is bright green and fork-tender, removing it from the pan and covering it will help it to continue to cook slowly, resulting in a crisp-tender texture. This dish is typically served warm, but works well served cool, too.

Serves 4
Hands-on time: 24 minutes
Total time: 24 minutes

1 cup vegetable oil, for frying

1 cup thinly sliced shallots (about 3 medium)

½ teaspoon kosher salt, plus more as needed

1 tablespoon olive oil

1 pound zucchini, halved lengthwise and cut into 3 x ½-inch spears

1 medium peach, halved, pitted, and cut into ½-inch-wide wedges

1 small serrano chile, thinly sliced (about 2 tablespoons)

¼ teaspoon freshly ground black pepper

¼ cup Peach Chutney (page 258)

2 teaspoons soy sauce

⅓ cup chopped fresh cilantro

1. Line a plate with paper towels and set it nearby. Heat the vegetable oil in a medium saucepan over medium heat to 275°F. Add the shallots and cook, stirring occasionally, for 5 minutes, or until browned and crispy. Remove from the oil with a slotted spoon and drain on the paper towels. Sprinkle with a generous pinch of salt.

2. Heat 1 teaspoon of the olive oil in a large skillet over medium-high heat. Add half the zucchini and cook, turning occasionally, for 4 minutes, or until charred. Transfer the zucchini to a large bowl and cover tightly to steam. Repeat with another 1 teaspoon of the olive oil and the remaining zucchini. Heat the remaining 1 teaspoon olive oil in the same skillet. Add the peach and cook, turning once, for 3 minutes, or until browned.

3. Toss together the zucchini, peach, serrano, the ½ teaspoon salt, the pepper, chutney, soy sauce, and cilantro in a serving bowl. Sprinkle with the shallots and serve.

Fried Green Tomatoes

with Homemade Ranch Dressing and Peach Hot Sauce

Fried green tomatoes are such a classic. These have a light but crunchy cornmeal batter, and we love the surprise element of peachy hot sauce. It adds a level of sophistication and a delectable sweetness that make these positively addictive.

A pie plate will work well as a shallow dish for breading the tomato rounds. Garnish the finished product with sea salt and, if you like, chopped fresh chives, and serve with Black-Eyed Peas (page 131), Peach Chutney (page 258), or Peach Ketchup (page 259). Better yet, add them to your BLP (page 109)!

Makes 15 pieces
Hands-on time: 20 minutes
Total time: 20 minutes

⅔ cup mayonnaise

⅓ cup plus ½ cup buttermilk

1½ teaspoons kosher salt,
plus more as needed

1 teaspoon freshly ground
black pepper

1 tablespoon Peach Vinegar
(page 270)

1 garlic clove, minced

1 tablespoon chopped
fresh chives

1 large egg

2 tablespoons Peach Hot
Sauce (page 271),
plus more for serving

¼ cup all-purpose flour

¾ cup fine yellow cornmeal

½ teaspoon garlic powder

3 firm green tomatoes
(about 1¼ pounds), sliced
into ¼-inch-thick rounds

Vegetable oil, for frying

1. Whisk together the mayonnaise, the ⅓ cup buttermilk, the ½ teaspoon of the salt, ½ teaspoon of the pepper, the vinegar, garlic, and chives in a small bowl. Cover the ranch dressing and chill until ready to use.

2. Whisk together the egg, the ½ cup buttermilk, and the hot sauce in a shallow dish. Place the flour in a separate shallow dish. Whisk together the cornmeal, remaining 1 teaspoon salt, remaining ½ teaspoon pepper, and the garlic powder in a third shallow dish.

3. Working in batches, dredge the tomato slices in the flour, then dip them in the egg mixture, then dredge them in the cornmeal mixture, shaking off any excess.

4. Fill a large deep skillet or Dutch oven with vegetable oil to a depth of ¼ inch. Heat the oil over medium-high heat to 350°F. Line a baking sheet with paper towels and set it nearby. Working in batches, fry the tomatoes in the hot oil for 2 minutes per side, or until golden brown. Drain on the paper towels; season with additional salt.

5. Serve the tomatoes warm, with the ranch dressing and hot sauce on top or alongside.

Buttermilk Biscuits

with The Peach Truck Signature Peach Jam

According to Stephen, there is nothing better in the world than a biscuit. This is a good recipe to have in your back pocket. It's got a golden, crunchy outside and a soft, buttery inside, the result of cutting the butter into cubes and pats, which creates layers of tender flakiness.

When you're forming the biscuits, cutting them into squares leaves no waste and eliminates the need for a cutter or for rerolling scraps. When folding and turning the dough to create layers, do it with a gentle hand so the dough doesn't become tough and overworked.

Makes 9 biscuits
Hands-on time: 15 minutes
Total time: 50 minutes

4½ cups all-purpose flour ground from soft red winter wheat (such as White Lily)

1 teaspoon baking soda

5 teaspoons baking powder

1½ teaspoons kosher salt

2 teaspoons sugar

1 cup (2 sticks) cold unsalted butter: ½ cup (1 stick) cut into ½-inch cubes, ½ cup (1 stick) sliced into ¼-inch-thick pats

1½ cups cold buttermilk

2 tablespoons salted butter or Sweet Peach Butter (page 256), melted

The Peach Truck Signature Peach Jam (page 263) or The Peach Truck Freezer Jam (page 253)

1. Preheat the oven to 450°F. Line a baking sheet with parchment paper.

2. Whisk together the flour, baking soda, baking powder, salt, and sugar in a large bowl. Add the butter cubes and pats, tossing to coat them in the flour. Cut in the butter with a pastry blender until broken down into pieces the size of peas. Make a well in the center of the flour mixture and add the buttermilk. Stir until just combined.

3. Turn out the dough onto a floured surface. Roll or pat it into a ½-inch-thick rectangle. Fold the dough into thirds lengthwise, then fold it into thirds crosswise. Turn the dough one quarter turn; roll or pat it into a ½-inch-thick rectangle. Repeat the folding process. Turn the dough one quarter turn again and repeat the rolling and folding process a third time.

4. Roll or pat the dough into a 9-inch square, ¾ inch thick. Cut the dough using a 2½-inch round cutter or use a sharp knife to cut the dough into 3-inch squares. Place the dough on the prepared baking sheet. Freeze the biscuits for 15 minutes.

5. Bake the biscuits for 20 minutes, or until golden brown.

6. Brush the tops with the melted butter. Serve warm, with peach jam.

Avocado-Peach Salad

with Green Goddess Dressing

Jessica grew up on her grandmother's homemade salad dressing—
a family heirloom that we always keep stocked in our kitchen.
Salad dressing should always be this way: homemade, a celebration of what you have on hand, a chance to get creative using your
pantry or garden herbs. This one is fresh and light and full of rich,
herby, garlicky flavors. It can be made three days ahead. It's the
perfect pairing with creamy avocados and sweet peaches on a bed
of butter lettuce.

Serves 4
Hands-on time: 10 minutes
Total time: 10 minutes

1 (7-ounce) head Bibb lettuce

2 medium peaches, pitted
  and sliced

2 avocados, pitted, peeled,
  and sliced

Green Goddess Dressing
  (recipe follows)

Flaky sea salt

Freshly ground black pepper

Divide the lettuce, peaches, and avocados among four plates.
Drizzle with the dressing, sprinkle with salt and pepper, and serve
with additional dressing on the side.

GREEN GODDESS DRESSING

Makes about 1 cup • Hands-on time: 5 minutes • Total time: 5 minutes

½ cup mayonnaise

⅓ cup buttermilk

½ cup chopped fresh basil

¼ cup chopped fresh chives

3 tablespoons chopped
   fresh tarragon

2 tablespoons fresh
   lemon juice

1 garlic clove, chopped

1 oil-packed anchovy fillet,
   chopped

¼ teaspoon kosher salt

¼ teaspoon freshly ground
   black pepper

Combine the mayonnaise, buttermilk, basil, chives, tarragon, lemon juice, garlic, anchovy, salt, and pepper in a blender or food processor. Blend until smooth. Store in an airtight container in the refrigerator for up to 3 days.

145

City House Peach Vinegar Salad

When we moved to Nashville, City House quickly became our spot. The classic Germantown brick house had recently been converted into a culinary playground for Nashville-native chef Tandy Wilson. There's a lot to say about Tandy—his passion for local produce, his forward-thinking business sense, his raw talent in the kitchen— but what sticks out most about him is his genuine kindness and interest in others. He loves people and humbly serves Nashville the most spectacular meals: pure, deceptively simple, and profoundly delicious.

This vinegar salad is incredibly well balanced: sweet and tangy and refreshing. You can prepare it up to three days ahead and serve it with cheese, salty pork, sausage, country ham, or stir it into salads as a dressing.

Serves 12

Hands-on time: 10 minutes

Total time: 3 hours 10 minutes

¾ cup distilled white vinegar

¾ cup apple cider vinegar

½ cup sugar

1½ tablespoons kosher salt

½ Vidalia onion, halved lengthwise and sliced crosswise into ¼-inch-thick pieces

2 jalapeños, halved lengthwise, seeded, and thinly sliced into half-moons

4 medium peaches

1. In a large jar with a tight-fitting lid, combine both vinegars, the sugar, ½ cup water, and the salt; seal the jar and shake until the sugar has dissolved. Add the onion and jalapeño and shake to combine. Let stand at room temperature for at least 2 hours or refrigerate overnight.

2. One hour before serving, pit and dice the peaches. Place them in a large bowl. Add the onion-jalapeño mixture to the bowl and toss well. Let stand for 1 hour before serving.

SUPPER

LOVE AROUND THE TABLE

We both grew up in homes where dinner was a ritual, a nightly family gathering during which everyone had a space to share incidents from their day. In Georgia, Stephen sat at a table filled with jokes and storytelling—and a subtle competition over who could get the biggest laughs—as well as a rotating roster of dinner guests that included anyone from a Little League buddy to an elderly neighbor. He loved hearing the stories of people whose backgrounds were different than his own. It was only later that Stephen realized that guests at the table were often invited over because they didn't have family to eat with. His parents never made a big deal about it; it was part of the normal rhythm of their home.

At Jessica's house in Seattle, dinner—orchestrated by her mother, who served up weeknight staples and salads from the family garden—was also a time of coming together. Jessica and her three brothers would slide into their spots at the table every night at six. It was there where she learned to formulate a story in her head and share it with humor and precision. Her parents used those dinners as teachable moments, encouraging Jessica and her siblings to taste everything, expand their young palates, and develop an appreciation for homegrown vegetables and a diversity of cuisines. "You've got to keep trying things—try that squash, try that green bean—educate your palate," her father would say. To this day, Jessica's eagerness to do and taste it all is his philosophy at work.

So many of our favorite memories have happened at the dinner table. There were those early days in Nashville as newlyweds, when on cool nights, we would move our table to the porch, watching the lightning bugs as we ate pasta and drank cheap wine with friends. Every year for Thanksgiving, we join Stephen's best friends, who come from points across the country to celebrate. We each make a dish, gather around the table, crack open bottles of wine and bourbon, and talk late into the night.

With three young kids, these days dinnertime can look a little more like a circus than intentional family time—but it's an evolving ritual that's important to all of us. Early in the evening, the kids sit around our kitchen island while we feed them dinner—Rainier and Wyatt in their high chairs, and Florence on a stool. It's a crazy mess, but fun, with lots of chatter, singing, and wiping up the floor. Someday we'll all sit at a table, but for now, the most important thing is letting our kids know that dinner is a time for us to be together and, later, as they get older, that this is a time when they can use their words, feel heard, and share their stories, too.

We create that space now with four-year-old Florence after we put her brothers to bed. We read books, sing songs, say good night to the sun and hello to the moon. We tell her when we have noticed her being kind or creative, and all the reasons we feel immense gratitude to be her parents.

However calm or hectic your dinner table, peaches—which seem right at home in breakfasts and desserts—might strike you as surprising for a main course, but the recipes here integrate them thoughtfully, in ways that feel just right. Heaped onto a fresh fish taco, glazing a pork chop, or infusing the ketchup on a burger, they add a note of ambrosial sweetness. For us, seeing a peach in a dish at the end of the day represents the culmination of a shared vision. For Jessica, cooking a main course is how she shows love—and that idea is threaded through these recipes. *Won't they go crazy for the white pizza? Wouldn't these sliders be fun for a party? Won't they be surprised to taste that peach grilled right up next to that steak?*

What we really hope is that you use these recipes to come together, whether it's with family, friends, or strangers. We think frequently of the Mr. Rogers quote: "Frankly, there isn't anyone you couldn't learn to love once you've heard their story," and we hope these dishes provide the framework for gatherings, and for new stories to be told.

Grilled Grouper Tacos

with Peach Pico

We can't resist fish tacos: light yet filling, they're our go-to warm-weather dinner. We love the communal aspect of this main dish—if you're having people over you can put out a spread that's easy to adapt for adults and kids alike. The grouper is simple and elegant, but any flaky white-fleshed fish would work well. Use angel hair cabbage, or thinly shred your own with a sharp knife or mandoline. The slaw and pico shouldn't be made more than several hours ahead, but the crema will keep for up to three days.

Serves 4
Hands-on time: 30 minutes
Total time: 30 minutes

CREMA

6 tablespoons sour cream

1 teaspoon grated lime zest

3 tablespoons fresh
    lime juice

1 garlic clove, minced

¼ teaspoon kosher salt

2 tablespoons chopped
    fresh cilantro

SLAW

2 tablespoons Peach Vinegar
    (page 270)

2 tablespoons extra-virgin
    olive oil

¼ teaspoon kosher salt

¼ cup chopped fresh cilantro

1 tablespoon finely diced
    seeded jalapeño

2 cups finely shredded
    cabbage

PICO

2 tablespoons fresh lime juice

½ teaspoon kosher salt

2 tablespoons finely diced
    seeded jalapeño

1¼ cups finely diced
    peaches (about 1 large)

¼ cup finely diced white
    onion

2 tablespoons chopped fresh
    cilantro

1.   To make the crema, whisk together the sour cream, lime zest, lime juice, garlic, salt, and cilantro in a small bowl. Cover and chill.

2.   To make the slaw, whisk together the vinegar, olive oil, salt, cilantro, and jalapeño in a medium bowl. Add the cabbage and toss well.

FISH

1 pound skinless grouper fillets

2 tablespoons olive oil

½ teaspoon chili powder

½ teaspoon ground cumin

¼ teaspoon kosher salt

8 (6-inch) corn tortillas, warmed

3. To make the pico, stir together the lime juice, salt, jalapeño, peaches, onion, and cilantro in a small bowl.

4. To grill the fish, heat a grill to medium (400°F) or heat a grill pan over medium-high heat.

5. Drizzle the fish with the olive oil. Sprinkle with the chili powder, cumin, and salt. Grill the fish for 6 minutes on each side, or until cooked through. Flake the fish.

6. Serve the fish in warm tortillas with the slaw, pico, and crema on top.

Seared Salmon

with Beet, Pistachio, and Watercress Salad

Jessica grew up in the Northwest, so her love of salmon is strong. In this dish, the white wine, peach, and herb reduction brings out the mellow tenderness of the fish, while the red and golden beets and the emerald-green watercress set off its pink hue beautifully.

Though you can use any type of salmon, wild caught will give you the best flavor and packs the most nutritional value. The beets can be cooked up to three days ahead. If you can't find watercress, substitute arugula, spinach, or mixed greens.

Serves 4

Hands-on time: 30 minutes

Total time: 1 hour 45 minutes

4 medium beets
   (1½ pounds), trimmed

2 tablespoons extra-virgin
   olive oil

4 cups watercress

½ cup chopped toasted
   pistachios

PEACH REDUCTION

1 teaspoon whole black
   peppercorns

2 whole cloves

2 thyme sprigs

½ cup dry white wine

2 teaspoons sugar

1½ cups chopped peaches,
   pureed (about 1 large)

¼ teaspoon kosher salt

DRESSING

¼ cup Peach Vinegar
   (page 270)

2 tablespoons stone-ground
   mustard

1 tablespoon honey

1 tablespoon minced shallot

¾ teaspoon kosher salt

½ teaspoon freshly ground
   black pepper

¼ cup extra-virgin olive oil

SALMON

4 (6-ounce) salmon fillets

¼ teaspoon kosher salt

¼ teaspoon freshly ground
   black pepper

2 tablespoons olive oil

1. Preheat the oven to 400°F.

2. Drizzle the beets with the olive oil. Wrap them tightly in aluminum foil. Bake for 1 hour 15 minutes, or until tender and easily pierced with a knife. Once cool enough to handle, peel the beets and cut them into wedges. Set aside.

3. To make the peach reduction, combine the peppercorns, cloves, and thyme sprigs in a piece of cheesecloth; gather the ends of the cheesecloth and tie them closed with butcher's twine to make a bundle. Combine the wine, sugar, and peach puree in a medium saucepan and add the cheesecloth bundle. Bring to a boil over medium-high heat; reduce the heat to medium-low and simmer for 15 minutes, or until reduced to ¾ cup. Remove the cheesecloth bundle. Stir in the salt.

4. To make the dressing, whisk together the vinegar, mustard, honey, shallot, salt, and pepper in a small bowl. While whisking, slowly drizzle in the olive oil and whisk until the dressing is emulsified. Set aside.

5. To cook the salmon, sprinkle with the salt and pepper. Heat the olive oil in a large nonstick skillet over medium-high heat. Add the salmon, skin side up, and cook for 4 minutes. Turn the salmon over and cook for 3 to 4 minutes more, until cooked through.

6. To serve, toss the beets with 2 tablespoons of the dressing in a large bowl. Add the watercress, pistachios, and remaining dressing and toss lightly. Spoon 3 tablespoons of the peach reduction onto each of four plates and smear it across the plates. Top each plate with a salmon fillet and a serving of the salad.

Sriracha Shrimp Skewers

with Collard-Peach Salad

We love cooking with skewers year-round—on the grill during the warmer months; under the broiler in fall and winter. It's a great way to combine flavors and balance protein with vegetables; as an added bonus, it also makes for a gorgeous presentation. Whenever we get our hands on fresh shrimp at the height of summer, this is what we make. If, like Jessica, you have a love affair with sriracha, you'll go crazy for this recipe, with its garlicky and ginger notes that pair nicely with the Asian-inspired green salad. Massaging the collards helps break down the fibers so they'll be tender and easier to enjoy raw.

Serves 4
Hands-on time: 20 minutes
Total time: 50 minutes

4 (10- to 12-inch) metal or wooden skewers

1 (12-ounce) bunch collard greens

2 cups thinly sliced red cabbage

2 teaspoons kosher salt

2 tablespoons sugar

2 cups matchstick-cut carrots

2 cups thinly sliced peaches (about 2 medium)

½ cup dry-roasted peanuts, chopped

½ teaspoon freshly ground black pepper

3 tablespoons plus ¼ cup vegetable oil

1. If using wooden skewers, place the skewers in water and let stand for 30 minutes.

2. Remove the collard leaves from their stems; discard the stems. Thinly slice the leaves. Combine the collards, cabbage, salt, and sugar in a large bowl. Massage with your hands for 1 minute to tenderize the greens. Let stand for 30 minutes. Drain any liquid that has collected in the bowl.

3. Add the carrots, peaches, peanuts, pepper, the 3 tablespoons vegetable oil, and the vinegar and toss to combine.

4. Heat a grill to medium (400°F) or heat a grill pan over medium-high heat.

(recipe continues)

¼ cup Peach Vinegar
(page 270)

¼ cup sriracha

2 garlic cloves, minced

1 tablespoon grated fresh
ginger

3 tablespoons fresh
lime juice

24 large shrimp (1 pound),
peeled and deveined

2 tablespoons toasted
sesame seeds

5. Whisk together the sriracha, garlic, ginger, lime juice, and the
¼ cup vegetable oil in a large bowl. Add the shrimp and toss to
coat. Drain the skewers and thread 6 shrimp onto each one.

6. Grill the shrimp for 2 to 3 minutes per side, until pink and no
longer translucent.

7. Sprinkle the skewers with the sesame seeds and serve
alongside the salad.

Grilled Pork Chops

with Peach Agrodolce, Grilled Corn Succotash, and Purple Potatoes

Talk about a colorful dish! The peaches and caramelized onion in the agrodolce, an Italian sweet and sour sauce, add a mouthwatering richness to the pork. Everything else can be made on the grill, so you'll truly feel like you're making the most of summer. Of course, any potato can be substituted here. And the agrodolce can be made up to three days ahead and is equally tasty on a sandwich or as part of an appetizer spread.

Serves 4
Hands-on time: 1 hour
Total time: 1 hour

AGRODOLCE

1 tablespoon extra-virgin olive oil

1 small sweet onion, thinly sliced (about 1 cup)

1 large peach, pitted and chopped (about 1½ cups)

¼ teaspoon red pepper flakes

1 bay leaf

¼ teaspoon fennel seeds

2 whole cloves

1 star anise pod

1 tablespoon apple cider vinegar

2 teaspoons brown sugar

Pinch of kosher salt

1. To make the agrodolce, heat the olive oil in a small saucepan over medium heat. Add the onion and cook for 5 minutes, or until softened. Add the peach, red pepper flakes, bay leaf, fennel seeds, cloves, star anise, vinegar, brown sugar, salt, and 1 tablespoon water. Reduce the heat to low, cover, and cook for 10 minutes, or until the onion and peach are very soft. Remove and discard the bay leaf, cloves, and star anise.

2. Heat a grill to medium (400°F).

3. To cook the potatoes and the pork chops, toss the potatoes with 2 tablespoons of the olive oil, ½ teaspoon of the salt, and ½ teaspoon of the black pepper. Place them in the center of two stacked sheets of heavy-duty aluminum foil; wrap them tightly in the foil. Place the foil pack on the grill; cook for 40 minutes, or until the potatoes are tender.

4. Meanwhile, drizzle the pork chops with the remaining 2 tablespoons olive oil and season with the remaining 1 teaspoon salt and 1 teaspoon black pepper. Grill the pork chops for 6 minutes per side, or until a meat thermometer inserted into the center reads 140°F.

(recipe continues)

POTATOES AND PORK CHOPS

1¾ pounds small purple potatoes, halved

4 tablespoons extra-virgin olive oil

1½ teaspoons kosher salt

1½ teaspoons freshly ground black pepper

4 (8-ounce) bone-in pork rib chops, each about 1 inch thick

SUCCOTASH

½ pound okra pods

1 cup cherry tomatoes

2 tablespoons extra-virgin olive oil

4 ears corn

1 cup cooked lima beans

2 green onions, chopped

¼ teaspoon kosher salt

¼ teaspoon freshly ground black pepper

4 tablespoons Savory Peach Butter (page 256), melted

2 teaspoons Peach Hot Sauce (page 271)

5. To make the succotash, toss the okra and tomatoes with 1 tablespoon of the olive oil in a large bowl. Brush the corn with the remaining 1 tablespoon olive oil. Grill the corn, turning occasionally, for 10 minutes, or until tender. Grill the okra and tomatoes in a grill basket, stirring occasionally, for 10 minutes, or until tender.

6. Cut the corn kernels from the cobs and transfer the corn to a large bowl. Halve the okra pods and add them to the bowl with the corn. Add the tomatoes, lima beans, green onions, salt, black pepper, 2 tablespoons of the peach butter, and the hot sauce.

7. Drizzle the remaining 2 tablespoons peach butter over the potatoes and toss well. Serve the pork chops topped with the agrodolce, with the potatoes and succotash alongside.

White Pizza

with Peach, Pancetta, and Chile

This pizza is absolutely delicious, with deep flavors from the ricotta and mozzarella (low moisture works best) paired with succulent slices of peach.

Do you have a pizza stone? It's not imperative, but we do find that it helps to create an evenly cooked crust with an airy texture. If you can't find pancetta, by all means substitute bacon. And if a Fresno chile isn't available, you can use jalapeño or red pepper flakes.

Serves 4
Hands-on time: 20 minutes
Total time: 40 minutes

1 pound prepared
  pizza dough

1 tablespoon fine cornmeal

2 ounces pancetta, diced

1 shallot, chopped

2 garlic cloves, minced

¼ cup heavy cream

¼ cup whole-milk
  ricotta cheese

¼ teaspoon kosher salt

⅛ teaspoon freshly ground
  black pepper

1 tablespoon chopped
  fresh basil, plus whole
  leaves for garnish

All-purpose flour, for dusting

4 ounces mozzarella cheese
  (preferably low moisture),
  shredded

1 medium peach, pitted and
  cut into wedges

1 Fresno chile, thinly sliced

1. Remove the pizza dough from the refrigerator and let stand for 30 minutes to come to room temperature.

2. Place a pizza stone in the oven and preheat the oven to 500°F. Line a baking sheet or pizza peel with parchment paper and sprinkle the parchment with the cornmeal.

3. Line a plate with paper towels and set it nearby. Cook the pancetta in a medium skillet over medium-high heat for 5 minutes, or until crispy. Drain on the paper towels, reserving the drippings in the skillet. Add the shallot and garlic to the drippings; cook for 2 minutes, or until softened. Add the cream and cook for 2 to 3 minutes, until slightly thickened.

4. Combine the ricotta, salt, pepper, and chopped basil in a small bowl.

5. Stretch or roll out the pizza dough on a lightly floured surface into a 12-inch circle. Transfer the dough to the prepared baking sheet. Spread the cream sauce evenly over the dough, leaving a ¼-inch border. Sprinkle the mozzarella over the sauce. Dollop the ricotta mixture over the mozzarella. Top with the peaches, chile slices, and pancetta.

6. Transfer the pizza, still on the parchment, to the hot pizza stone. Bake for 12 to 14 minutes, until the crust is browned and the cheese is bubbling. Remove the pizza from the oven and let stand for 5 minutes.

7. Garnish with the basil leaves, slice, and serve.

Grilled Hanger Steak

with Grilled Peach Halves, Scallions, and Chile-Lime Butter

In our opinion, nothing signals summer like the moment you find yourself grilling a peach. You can use skirt or flank steak here, and can make the butter up to a week ahead. And if you're trying to cut down on red meat, rest assured, this approach would work just as well with a fresh tuna or swordfish steak, just reduce the cooking time to three or four minutes per side.

Serves 4
Hands-on time: 30 minutes
Total time: 30 minutes

½ cup (1 stick) salted butter, at room temperature

1 tablespoon minced canned chipotle chile in adobo sauce

½ teaspoon adobo sauce (from the can)

1 teaspoon lime zest

2 pounds hanger steak, trimmed

4 tablespoons olive oil

1¼ teaspoons kosher salt

1¼ teaspoons freshly ground black pepper

2 large peaches, halved and pitted

2 bunches green onions (about 12)

1. Stir together the butter, chipotle, adobo sauce, and lime zest in a small bowl. Cover and chill until ready to serve.

2. Heat a grill to high (600°F) or heat a grill pan over high heat.

3. Drizzle the steak with 2 tablespoons of the olive oil and sprinkle with 1 teaspoon of the salt and 1 teaspoon of the pepper. Drizzle the peaches and green onions with the remaining 2 tablespoons oil and sprinkle with the remaining ¼ teaspoon salt and ¼ teaspoon pepper. Grill the steak for 8 minutes, turning occasionally, until a meat thermometer reads 125°F for medium-rare. Grill the peaches and green onions, turning once, for 3 to 4 minutes, until tender and charred. Let the steak rest for 10 minutes before slicing.

4. Slice the steak against the grain and serve with the peaches, green onions, and a generous smear of the chile-lime butter.

Pearl Couscous

with Chickpeas, Eggplant, and Peaches

This is our only vegetarian main dish, so we gave it everything we got. Man, is it good! Pearl couscous with kalamata olives, chickpeas, and generous slices of red onion and peach becomes a bowl of irresistible goodness. The tahini adds depth of flavor and a lovely creaminess. This dish is great cold, warm, or at room temperature, and you can make it up to one day ahead.

Serves 6
Hands-on time: 15 minutes
Total time: 35 minutes

1 pound peaches, pitted and cut into ½-inch-thick wedges (about 3 medium)

1 small red onion, cut into ½-inch-thick wedges

1 (1-pound) eggplant, cut into 1-inch cubes

1 (15½-ounce) can chickpeas, rinsed, drained, and patted dry

4 thyme sprigs

8 tablespoons extra-virgin olive oil

1 teaspoon smoked paprika

¼ teaspoon cayenne pepper

2 teaspoons kosher salt

1½ teaspoons freshly ground black pepper

3 cups vegetable broth

2½ cups pearl couscous

½ cup chopped pitted kalamata olives

½ cup chopped fresh parsley

½ cup chopped fresh mint

1 teaspoon lemon zest

2 tablespoons fresh lemon juice

2 tablespoons tahini

1. Preheat the oven to 425°F.

2. Toss together the peaches, onion, eggplant, chickpeas, thyme sprigs, 5 tablespoons of the olive oil, the paprika, cayenne, 1 teaspoon of the salt, and 1 teaspoon of the black pepper in a large bowl. Divide the mixture between two rimmed baking sheets and spread into a single layer. Bake for 20 minutes, or until the vegetables are tender. Remove the thyme sprigs.

3. Meanwhile, bring the broth to a boil in a large saucepan. Add the couscous, cover, and reduce the heat to maintain a simmer. Cook for 8 to 10 minutes, until the liquid has been absorbed and the couscous is al dente.

4. In a large serving bowl, toss together the couscous, roasted vegetables and peaches, olives, parsley, mint, lemon zest, lemon juice, tahini, remaining 3 tablespoons oil, remaining 1 teaspoon salt, and remaining ½ teaspoon pepper. Serve warm, chilled, or at room temperature.

Chicken Sliders, Three Ways

You're bound to like one, if not all three, of the takes on chicken sliders in this recipe, which we love putting out for a gathering where you have a lot of different palates to please. If you're hosting a party, save yourself some day-of hassle and cook the jerk and BBQ chicken ahead, then warm them before serving. These all look beautiful on a serving platter and, as an added bonus, are easy for little hands.

FRIED CHICKEN SLIDERS

Makes 8 sliders • Hands-on time: 25 minutes • Total time: 1 hour 25 minutes

4 boneless, skinless chicken thighs (about 1 pound)

½ cup buttermilk

½ cup mayonnaise

1 tablespoon Peach Hot Sauce (page 271)

1 garlic clove, minced

1 cup all-purpose flour

1 teaspoon kosher salt, plus more as needed

1 teaspoon freshly ground black pepper

Vegetable oil, for frying

8 slider buns

8 small lettuce leaves

8 thin slices red onion

8 thin slices Pickled Peaches (page 272)

1. Cut each chicken thigh in half. Place them in a bowl or zip-top bag; add the buttermilk and toss well. Cover and chill for 1 hour.

2. Stir together the mayonnaise, hot sauce, and garlic in a small bowl. Cover and chill until ready to use.

3. Whisk together the flour, ½ teaspoon of the salt, and ½ teaspoon of the pepper in a shallow dish. Drain the chicken from the buttermilk, discarding the buttermilk. Sprinkle the chicken with the remaining ½ teaspoon salt and ½ teaspoon pepper. Working in batches, dredge the chicken in the flour mixture.

4. Fill a large deep skillet or Dutch oven with vegetable oil to a depth of 1 inch. Heat the oil over medium-high heat to 350°F. Line a baking sheet with paper towels and set it nearby. Working in batches, fry the chicken in the oil for 3 minutes per side, or until cooked through. Drain on the paper towels and season with salt.

5. Spread the cut side of the buns with the mayonnaise mixture. Top each with a piece of chicken, a lettuce leaf, a slice of onion, and a slice of pickled peach; serve.

JERK CHICKEN SLIDERS

Makes 8 sliders • Hands-on time: 15 minutes • Total time: 1 hour 5 minutes

2 green onions, finely chopped

2 teaspoons ground allspice

2 teaspoons dried thyme

1 teaspoon cayenne pepper

1 teaspoon kosher salt

½ teaspoon freshly ground black pepper

½ teaspoon freshly grated nutmeg

2 tablespoons brown sugar

4 boneless, skinless chicken thighs (about 1 pound)

8 slider buns

½ cup Peach Chutney (page 258)

1. Combine the green onions, allspice, thyme, cayenne, salt, black pepper, nutmeg, and brown sugar in a bowl or zip-top bag. Add the chicken and rub the spice mixture all over. Let stand at room temperature for 30 minutes, or cover and chill for up to 24 hours.

2. Preheat the oven to 425°F. Line a baking sheet with aluminum foil.

3. Place the chicken on the prepared baking sheet and bake for 20 minutes, or until cooked through. Let cool slightly; shred the chicken.

4. Divide the shredded chicken among the buns, top each with 1 tablespoon of the chutney, and serve.

(recipe continues)

BBQ CHICKEN SLIDERS

Makes 8 sliders • Hands-on time: 15 minutes • Total time: 35 minutes

4 boneless, skinless chicken thighs (about 1 pound)

¾ teaspoon kosher salt

¾ teaspoon freshly ground black pepper

½ cup Peach Bourbon BBQ Sauce (page 255)

2 tablespoons mayonnaise

1 tablespoon distilled white vinegar

⅛ teaspoon celery seeds

1 cup shredded cabbage

¼ cup shredded carrot

8 slider buns

8 dill pickle slices

1. Preheat the oven to 425°F. Line a baking sheet with aluminum foil.

2. Put the chicken in a large bowl and season with ½ teaspoon of the salt and ½ teaspoon of the pepper. Pour ¼ cup of the BBQ sauce over the chicken and toss to coat. Place the chicken on the prepared baking sheet and bake for 20 minutes, or until cooked through. Let cool slightly; shred the chicken and place it in a medium bowl.

3. Whisk together the mayonnaise, vinegar, celery seeds, remaining ¼ teaspoon salt, and remaining ¼ teaspoon pepper in a medium bowl. Add the cabbage and carrot and toss to coat.

4. Warm the remaining ¼ cup BBQ sauce in a small saucepan. Add it to the bowl with the shredded chicken and toss to coat.

5. Divide the shredded chicken evenly among the buns. Top each slider with a pickle slice and some of the slaw and serve.

Sticky Peach-Glazed Ribs

Ideal for a backyard barbecue, these are easy to prep ahead: you can make the sauce and precook the ribs, and simply toss them on the grill when your guests arrive. Roll up your sleeves! The sweet-and-sticky glaze makes a mess, but it is totally worth it. Serve with all the trimmings, or old-school, with white bread and pickles.

Serves 4–6

Hands-on time: 1 hour 30 minutes

Total time: 3 hours 30 minutes

RIB RUB

2 tablespoons brown sugar

2 tablespoons kosher salt

1 tablespoon smoked paprika

2 teaspoons granulated garlic

2 teaspoons freshly ground black pepper

RIBS

2 (16-ounce) beers of your choice

6 to 8 celery stalks

1 large onion, cut into large chunks

7 pounds pork ribs

PEACH BBQ SAUCE

4 or 5 medium peaches, pitted and cut into large cubes

2 tablespoons vegetable oil

2½ cups finely minced Vidalia onion (about 1 large)

3 garlic cloves, minced

1. Preheat the oven to 275°F.

2. To make the rub, combine all the rub ingredients in a small bowl and set aside.

3. To make the ribs, pour the beers into a large roasting pan and place the celery and onion in the pan. Season the racks of ribs liberally on both sides with the rib rub and place them in the pan, elevated on a rack if you have one. Cover the pan with parchment paper, then cover tightly with aluminum foil. Bake for 2 hours.

4. Meanwhile, to make the sauce, puree the peaches in a blender until smooth. You should have about 3 cups of puree. Set aside.

5. Heat a large saucepan over medium heat. Add the vegetable oil, onion, and garlic. Cover the pan and cook, stirring occasionally, for 10 minutes. Stir in the peach puree, brown sugar, vinegar, Worcestershire, and red pepper flakes. Bring to a boil, then reduce the heat to maintain a low simmer. Cook, stirring regularly, for 30 to 40 minutes, until the sauce has reduced and thickened. Remove from the heat and stir in the mustard. Taste and add salt if needed. If preparing in advance, let cool completely and transfer the sauce to an airtight glass or other nonreactive container and store in the refrigerator for up to 1 month.

6. Once the ribs have cooked for 2 hours, take the pan out of the oven and carefully remove the racks of ribs from the pan. At this point, you can either refrigerate the ribs to cook later—let them cool first—or continue straight to the grill.

1½ cups lightly packed
brown sugar

½ cup apple cider vinegar

¼ cup Worcestershire sauce

½ teaspoon red pepper flakes

3 tablespoons prepared
mustard

Kosher salt

7. Heat a grill to medium (400°F).

8. Depending on the size of the grill and your serving preference, you can cut the racks of ribs into smaller sections or leave them whole. Liberally coat the ribs with the sauce and place them on the grill. Cook, monitoring the ribs as they cook, turning them over every few minutes and applying more sauce, until they are nicely browned and caramelized. Since the ribs were fully cooked in the oven, this process will only take 10 to 15 minutes on the grill.

The 404 Kitchen Peach Roasted Chicken

The 404 Kitchen in Nashville's Gulch neighborhood has a James Beard Best New Restaurant nomination under its belt, and its whiskey bar was deemed one of America's best by *Travel + Leisure*. Chef Matt Bolus is to thank, with his classic European menu known for seasonal ingredients and a modern touch. The roasted chicken he dreamed up for us truly celebrates the art of cooking and the whole sensory-laden experience of making a meal. So grab a glass of wine and enjoy the process: roasting peaches, onions, and herbs with the chicken in the pan; pureeing them into an incredibly flavorful peach sauce; then drizzling it over the chicken and tomato salad. Ah! This tomato salad! It's light but has incredible depth of flavor, thanks to the deliriously brilliant addition of Marcona almonds.

Serves 4

Hands-on time: 20 minutes

Total time: 1 hour 30 minutes

ROAST CHICKEN

1 (3- to 3½-pound) whole chicken

Kosher salt

Freshly ground black pepper

1 medium yellow onion, quartered

1 garlic clove

4 medium peaches, halved and pitted

6 thyme sprigs

1 rosemary sprig

1 fresh bay leaf

2 tablespoons fresh lemon juice, plus more for the sauce if needed

1. To roast the chicken, preheat the oven to 375°F.

2. Season the cavity of the chicken with salt and pepper. Stuff the cavity with half the onion, the garlic, 1 peach, and half the thyme and rosemary sprigs. Truss the chicken with butcher's twine.

3. Put the remaining 3 peaches, onion, thyme and rosemary sprigs, and bay leaf in a roasting pan. Season the top (breast side) of the chicken with salt and pepper. Lay the chicken on the peaches and onions, breast side down.

4. Pour the lemon juice over the back of the chicken and season it with salt and pepper.

5. Cover the roasting pan with aluminum foil and roast the chicken for 1 hour.

(recipe continues)

TOMATO SALAD

1 quart cherry tomatoes, halved

¾ cup coarsely chopped Marcona almonds, plus more if desired

½ ounce fresh ginger, peeled and finely chopped

1 shallot, finely chopped and rinsed

1½ teaspoons kosher salt

8 twists of freshly ground black pepper

¼ cup extra-virgin olive oil

¼ cup finely chopped fresh parsley

6. To make the tomato salad, toss the tomatoes, almonds, ginger, and shallot together in a large glass bowl. Season with the salt and pepper. Let the salad sit at room temperature while you finish the chicken.

7. At the end of the first hour of cooking, remove the roasting pan from the oven, remove the foil, and carefully flip the chicken. Put the chicken back in the oven, uncovered, breast side up, and roast for 20 to 30 minutes more until the chicken is cooked through to 165°F.

8. When the chicken is cooked, carefully remove it from the roasting pan, cut the leg trussing, and empty the stuffed contents into the roasting pan. Allow the chicken to rest while you prepare the sauce.

9. Remove all the thyme and rosemary sprigs and bay leaf from the roasting pan and discard them. Transfer the remaining contents of the pan to a blender. *Carefully*, with a towel over the top of the blender and starting on the lowest speed, blend the ingredients, gradually picking up speed until the blender is on high and the ingredients form a smooth sauce.

10. Pass the sauce through a strainer, taste, and adjust the seasoning with salt, pepper, and extra lemon juice as needed.

11. Toss the tomatoes with the olive oil and parsley and lay them all out on a platter.

12. Cut the breasts off the chicken and cut each breast into 2 pieces. Cut the legs from the chicken (not forgetting the oyster) and cut the thighs from the drumsticks. Put all 8 pieces of chicken on top of the tomato salad. Pour the peach sauce over the top and serve.

Sean Brock's Double Cheeseburger

with Peach Ketchup

Husk, the award-winning Nashville restaurant founded by Sean Brock, is known for many things, but chief among them is its cheeseburger—and the fact that Brock has been willing to share his celebrated recipe is a true gift. Stephen had been on a quest to re-create it after too many backyard barbecues disappointed him with fat, flavorless patties. But now we don't have to live that way.

This diner-style double-stacked creation uses thin patties with ground bacon, cooked on super-high heat. This is exactly the kind of burger you want to eat, with notes of bacon and tangy sweet Peach Ketchup as the small but mighty star. Grinding your own meat can be rewarding, but if you don't have a grinder in your kitchen, ask your butcher to do it for you. We repeat: this is the absolute best burger; the best burger there is.

Serves 10
Hands-on time: 40 minutes
Total time: 40 minutes

3 pounds boneless chuck roast

12 ounces flank steak

3 ounces slab bacon (we prefer Benton's)

3 tablespoons unsalted butter, at room temperature

10 hamburger buns

1 cup shaved white onion

20 slices American cheese

1¼ cups Peach Ketchup (page 259)

1. Grind the chuck, flank steak, and bacon through a meat grinder fitted with the large die into a large bowl. Mix gently to combine. Grind half the mixture again, this time using the small die. Mix the two together.

2. Portion the meat mixture into twenty 3-ounce balls. If not cooking the burgers right away, arrange them on a rimmed baking sheet, cover tightly with plastic wrap, and refrigerate.

3. Generously butter the tops and bottoms of the buns. Toast them on a griddle until golden brown. Transfer them to a rimmed baking sheet, toasted sides up, and set aside.

(recipe continues)

4.   Heat two 12-inch cast-iron skillets over high heat until very hot and just barely beginning to smoke, 2 to 3 minutes. Divide the balls of meat between the two skillets, smashing each down with a spatula to flatten them into patties and create a dark brown crust. When the patties are charred, about 2 minutes, turn them over and cook for 2 minutes more for medium. Divide the onion among 10 of the patties. Place a slice of the cheese on each patty and allow it to melt, about 30 seconds. Stack the patties without the onion on top of the patties with the onion. Remove them from the heat. Transfer the burger stacks to a wire rack and let them rest for 1 minute.

5.   Smear both sides of the buns with Peach Ketchup. Add the burger patties and cover with the tops of the buns. Serve at once.

DRINKS

PORCH SITTIN'

Our home in Nashville has two porches: a front and a back. Screened in and facing west, the back porch is where we go to tuck away in stillness. We sit there in the mornings while the sun rises at our backs. At night, after our three little ones are in bed, one of our favorite things to do is light a fire out there and sip a glass of bourbon. It feels like a safe environment, cloistered from the rest of the world. It's a setting that's played host to so many conversations—between us, about our dreams for our family, and with our friends. After a long, eventful day—especially during peach season—there's nowhere we'd rather be.

With a dormant period that stretches for nearly half the year, peach trees can actually teach us quite a bit about the importance of stillness, especially in a world that's constantly seeking to distract us. Peach orchards fall quiet in the winter, becoming different scenes entirely from the daily bustle that characterizes their summer months. But it's during that important downtime that the trees are replenishing themselves, sucking up nutrients and preparing to bloom. In a way, that kind of recharging is exactly what we're doing when we sit on the back porch—taking a minute to slow down, appreciate what we're working hard for, and take care of ourselves.

Our front porch, however, is an entirely different story.

An open-air space with plenty of chairs, our front porch is a party. On those hot summer evenings, it's a place to unwind with the kids while drinking lemonade and listening to the chorus of the neighborhood in the background—the chatter of passersby, the screech of sidewalk chalk, the hum of car engines. As cosmopolitan as it has become, Nashville still feels like a big small town. It's not unusual for a friend to be driving by our house, see us on the front porch, pull over, and join us. Before long, we're talking late into the night and mixing up peach margaritas long after we've put the kids to sleep.

During those long peach-season days, we're powered by sparkling water, iced teas, and lemonades. At night, bourbon is the base of our respective drinks of choice—an old-fashioned for Jessica, and a hard-to-find bourbon, on the rocks (with a good, solid ice cube that melts slowly), for Stephen.

The recipes in this section offer a fruit-forward take on the Southern tradition of refreshing sweet teas and ades. At the same time, they demonstrate that peaches can stand up to a variety of liquors, mixers, and embellishments. They're inventive additions to a new generation of artisanal cocktails, which have enlivened the Nashville culinary landscape in the same way they have other food cities, appearing in frothy Peach Pisco Sours, Peach Mules, light spritzers, and granitas.

The reality is, in the South, the summer days are hot and long. It's a gift, for sure, but they can feel exhausting. Sitting on a porch—alone or in good company—and sipping a refreshing drink slowly feels like a reward. There's a celebratory element to it. People work hard here, but they enjoy one another, and there's a communal spirit of working and living in and loving Nashville. And let's not forget that the South is full of storytellers, steeped in the tradition of sitting around, enjoying a cold drink together, and listening and laughing while someone tells a spellbinding story at the end of the day.

Minty Peach Lemonade

With mint sprigs that bring this lemonade to new heights, this liba-
tion requires a bit of patience, but it is worth it! It's truly the
epitome of refreshment. Make it ahead of time for a hot weekend,
or if you're expecting guests. You'll get so much mileage out of it
once you do—you can use it as a base for cocktails, mix it with
Peach Sweet Tea (opposite page) for a Peach Arnold Palmer, or
freeze it in ice pop molds for a summer treat.

Serves 6

Hands-on time: 15 minutes

Total time: 3 hours 45 minutes

4 medium peaches:
  3 chopped (about 3 cups),
  1 sliced, for garnish

¾ cup sugar

**2 to 4 mint sprigs, plus more
  for garnish**

1 cup fresh lemon juice

Ice, for serving

1. Combine the chopped peaches, sugar, mint sprigs, and 4
cups water in a medium saucepan. Bring to a boil over medium-
high heat; reduce the heat to medium-low and simmer for 3
minutes. Let cool for 30 minutes. Remove and discard the mint
sprigs.

2. Transfer the peach mixture into a blender and blend until
smooth. Refrigerate for 3 hours or up to overnight.

3. Strain the peach mixture through a fine-mesh sieve; discard
the solids. Stir in the lemon juice.

4. Serve the lemonade over ice, garnished with the peach slices
and additional mint sprigs.

Peach Sweet Tea

Jessica's mother is from Texas, and two of the Lone Star traditions she brought into the family's home in Seattle were banana pudding and sweet tea. Jessica remembers how much of a to-do the making of tea would be, as her mother steeped bags in a big jar on their porch for three days. Few drinks are more refreshing on hot summer days, so we definitely wanted to include our own take on it here.

Makes about 8 cups
Hands-on time: 15 minutes
Total time: 15 minutes

10 black tea bags

1 lemon, washed and sliced

1 (2-inch) piece fresh ginger, peeled and smashed

4 cups ice

1½ cups Peach Simple Syrup (page 266)

1. Place the tea bags, lemon slices, and ginger in a large pitcher.

2. Bring 4 cups water to a boil in a medium saucepan. Pour the water into the pitcher; let steep for 7 minutes.

3. Remove the tea bags, lemon slices, and ginger. Add the ice and stir until it melts. Stir in the peach syrup.

4. Pour into ice-filled glasses and serve.

Peach Sweet Tea
(page 189)

Minty Peach Lemonade (page 188)

Sparkling Peach Sangria (page 198)

Peach Mule

We love a classic Moscow Mule. Adding a peach creates a fizzy blend that tastes like summer. You can swap the vodka for Fresh Georgia Peach Bourbon (page 196) if you'd prefer. If you don't have the traditional copper mug, a Collins glass or julep cup will work just fine.

Makes 1 cocktail
Hands-on time: 5 minutes
Total time: 5 minutes

2 lime wedges

½ cup peach slices
   (about 1 small)

Ice

¼ cup Peach Vodka
   (page 197) (2 ounces)

¾ cup ginger beer (6 ounces)

Squeeze 1 lime wedge into a copper mug or Collins glass. Place the squeezed lime and the peach slices in the mug and muddle them. Fill the mug with ice. Pour the vodka and ginger beer into the mug; stir. Serve garnished with the remaining lime wedge.

Peach Basil Spritzer

During our five-month travel stint after peach season in 2013, our venture through Italy taught us about the beauty of an afternoon spritz. While in Venice, we met up with a traveler whom we'd befriended in India, and his Italian family welcomed us into their home. Every afternoon, their friends would gather in the plaza and sip on spritzes made of prosecco and Campari. It was a part of the culture we're always happy to relive through this recipe. The homemade peach shrub for this clean, refreshing spritzer will keep for up to two weeks in the refrigerator.

Serves 16; makes 2 cups shrub
Hands-on time: 10 minutes
Total time: 2 hours 40 minutes

2 cups chopped peaches (about 2 medium)

2 cups sugar

1 teaspoon whole black peppercorns

¼ cup chopped fresh basil, plus basil sprigs for garnish (optional)

½ cup white wine vinegar

Ice

8 cups club soda or seltzer

1. Combine the peaches, sugar, peppercorns, chopped basil, and 2 tablespoons water in a medium saucepan. Bring to a boil over medium-high heat, stirring until the sugar has dissolved. Reduce the heat to medium-low and simmer until the peaches begin to break down, about 4 minutes. Remove from the heat; mash the peaches with a potato masher. Let cool for 30 minutes.

2. Pour the peach mixture through a fine-mesh sieve; discard the solids. Stir in the vinegar. Cover and chill for at least 2 hours.

3. For each drink, pour 2 tablespoons of the peach shrub into an ice-filled glass. Top with ½ cup of the club soda. Garnish with a basil sprig, if desired, and serve. If you're not using all the shrub immediately, store it in an airtight container in the refrigerator for 2 to 3 weeks.

Peach Prosecco Granita

Growing up, Jessica and her little brother, Tim, did work around the neighborhood for neighbors when they were away—collecting mail, watering the gardens, feeding the cats. After finishing a job, they'd race to 7-Eleven on their bikes to spend their earnings. They always rewarded themselves with Slurpees—no matter what. It was a great first taste of entrepreneurship, and perhaps it's no coincidence that they both wound up starting their own businesses. Jessica remembers everything about that slushy experience—the size of the cup in her small hands, the colorful lineup of flavors, the oversized straw. This Peach Prosecco Granita is a grown-up take on those Slurpees—a frozen cocktail that doubles as dessert (and with no artificial flavors).

Serves 12

Hands-on time: 10 minutes

Total time: 5 hours 10 minutes, plus overnight freezing time

1½ **pounds peaches, pitted and chopped (about 5 cups)**

1 **cup sugar**

2 **mint sprigs**

Pinch of kosher salt

2 **tablespoons fresh lemon juice**

1½ **cups prosecco**

1. Combine half the peaches, the sugar, mint sprigs, salt, and ¼ cup water in a medium saucepan. Bring to a boil over medium-high heat, stirring until the sugar has dissolved. Remove the mint sprigs. Pour the hot syrup into a food processor or blender. Add the lemon juice and the remaining peaches; puree until smooth.

2. Pour the puree into a 9-inch square baking dish. Stir in the prosecco. Cover and freeze for 3 hours. Stir with a fork. Cover and freeze for 3 hours more, scraping the mixture with a fork every hour or so, until the mixture is frozen and scraped into fluffy, icy crystals. Cover and freeze for 8 hours more before serving.

Fresh Georgia Peach Bourbon

Peach-infused bourbon tastes like a robust toast to the South. We like to use peaches that are almost overripe and a high-proof bourbon so that the sweetness of the peach really cuts any bite. The final product is smooth and just sweet enough. Exceptional on the rocks, this can be substituted in virtually any bourbon cocktail—including a Burger Up's Peach Truck Old-Fashioned (page 202).

Makes about 3 cups

Hands-on time: 10 minutes

Total time: 10 minutes, plus 7 to 10 days steeping time

3 or 4 medium peaches, pitted and quartered

2 tablespoons sugar

2 whole cloves

3 allspice berries

1 (750ml) bottle good-quality bourbon

Place the peaches in a large glass jar. Add the sugar, cloves, and allspice, then pour in the bourbon and seal the jar tightly. Place out of direct sunlight and let steep for 7 to 10 days. Once infused, strain the bourbon through a piece of cheesecloth into an airtight decanter or jar and discard the peaches. The infused bourbon will keep indefinitely.

Peach Vodka

Vodka is a fantastic vehicle for both the color and sweet flavor of a ripe peach. It soaks up all the juicy substance in a week. In this recipe, you can determine if you've let the vodka steep long enough to absorb the flavors by testing a small amount with seltzer. If you can taste the peach, the vodka is ready for all sorts of cocktails.

Makes about 3 cups

Hands-on time: 10 minutes

Total time: 10 minutes, plus 7 to 10 days steeping time

3 or 4 medium peaches, pitted and quartered

2 tablespoons sugar

2 whole cloves

3 allspice berries

1 (750ml) bottle good-quality vodka

Place the peaches in a large glass jar. Add the sugar, cloves, and allspice, then pour in the vodka and seal the jar tightly. Place out of direct sunlight and let steep for 7 to 10 days. Once infused, strain the vodka through a piece of cheesecloth into an airtight decanter or jar and discard the peaches. The infused vodka will keep indefinitely.

Sparkling Peach Sangria

We love sangria for any time of day, really, but especially for a brunch. Made in advance, it's the perfect balance of refreshment and spirits. This recipe is a little different, in that it makes a sangria concentrate whose strength you can control with the amount of seltzer added to it. Serve over ice.

Makes about 2 gallons
Hands-on time: 15 minutes
Total time: 15 minutes
plus overnight

2 (750 ml) bottles rosé wine

2 cups peach-flavored brandy

2 cups vodka or Peach Vodka (page 197)

1 (12-ounce) can frozen lemonade concentrate

1 cup Peach Simple Syrup (page 266)

2 lemons, washed and sliced

6 medium peaches

4 (1L) bottles plain seltzer

Ice

Fresh mint, for garnish

1. Combine the wine, brandy, vodka, lemonade concentrate, peach syrup, and sliced lemons in a gallon-size glass jar. Stir to combine. Pit and slice 4 of the peaches and add them to the jar. Cover and refrigerate overnight.

2. Pit and slice the remaining 2 peaches. For each drink, pour ¼ cup of the sangria mix and ¼ cup of the seltzer into a glass filled with ice. Garnish with the mint and sliced peaches.

Peach Pisco Sour

This cocktail turns out quite elegantly, thanks to its frothy egg white lather. Make sure it's especially creamy by shaking the ingredients first without the ice. Add one to two tablespoons more peach syrup, if you'd like a sweeter drink, and serve—we like it with the Marché Peach Tartine (page 86)!—in a dainty glass.

Makes 1 cocktail
Hands-on time: 5 minutes
Total time: 5 minutes

1 large egg white

¼ cup pisco (2 ounces)

2 tablespoons Peach Simple Syrup (page 266)

2 tablespoons fresh lime juice

Ice

Combine the egg whites, pisco, peach syrup, and lime juice in a cocktail shaker. Shake vigorously for 20 seconds; add ice to fill the shaker. Shake for 10 seconds. Strain into a cocktail glass and serve.

Peninsula's Gin and Peach Tonic (page 205)

Burger Up's Peach Truck Old-Fashioned (page 202)

Peach Pisco Sour (page 199)

Van Winkle's
Bourbon Peach
Cocktail (page
204)

Burger Up's
Peach Truck
Margarita
(page 203)

Burger Up's Peach Truck Old-Fashioned

The establishment that's largely to thank for the growth of Nashville's 12 South neighborhood, Burger Up sources local ingredients for its extensive menu, which runs the gamut from burgers topped with Benton's bacon to bison and quinoa patties. They were the first restaurant to use our name as a descriptor for a dish, and it felt so monumental that we nabbed a copy of the menu and have it to this day. The inspiration for this cocktail? An old-fashioned, of course—classic and boozy, with fresh peach muddled in for the ideal touch of sweetness.

Makes 1 cocktail

Hands-on time: 5 minutes

Total time: 5 minutes

½ **ounce simple syrup**

2 slices peach

2 dashes peach bitters

3 dashes Angostura bitters

2 ounces bourbon (we like Belle Meade)

Ice

1. To make the simple syrup, bring a 1:1 ratio of granulated sugar and water to a boil over medium-high heat, stirring until the sugar dissolves. Remove from the heat and cool completely. Refrigerate for up to 1 month.

2. Muddle the peach slices, bitters, and simple syrup in a rocks glass. Add the bourbon and ice; stir. Serve immediately.

Burger Up's Peach Truck Margarita

This cocktail, also on the menu at the legendary Burger Up, is delicious and dangerous, as most margaritas are. It's super drinkable and refreshing, and while we love it on the rocks, we've been known to blend these up on a hot summer night, too. The spicy kick of the jalapeño plays nicely off the peach in a drink that would also go wonderfully well with our Sweet and Spicy Empanadas (page 82).

Makes 1 cocktail
Hands-on time: 5 minutes
Total time: 5 minutes

Sugar, for rimming the glass

Lime wedge

2 slices peach

1 ounce simple syrup (see previous page)

2 dashes peach bitters

2 ounces jalapeño tequila (we like Tanteo)

1 ounce fresh lime juice

1 cup ice

1 strip orange peel (peeled with a vegetable peeler)

1. Pour some sugar onto a shallow plate or saucer. Rub the rim of a glass with the lime wedge and dip the rim in the sugar to coat.

2. Muddle the peach slices, simple syrup, and bitters in a cocktail shaker. Add the tequila, lime juice, and ice. Cover and shake for 15 seconds.

3. Pour the cocktail into the prepared glass. Twist the orange peel over the glass and drop it into the cocktail. Serve immediately.

Van Winkle's Bourbon Peach Cocktail

In Stephen's opinion, Pappy Van Winkle bourbon is the best there is. It's incredibly hard to find, so when Sissy, wife of Julian, the president of the company, came across our peaches and ordered a box, we were, frankly, starstruck. We soon developed a friendship, and are honored when they place their order every summer. We're even more honored that they contributed this recipe, a favorite of Julian's, which was created by a bartender in New York.

You can find Demerara syrup in many grocery stores, but you can also make your own by combining ½ cup Demerara sugar and ½ cup water in a small saucepan and bringing it to a boil over medium-high heat, stirring until the sugar has dissolved. Let cool. Store in an airtight container in the refrigerator for up to one month.

Makes 1 cocktail
Hands-on time: 5 minutes
Total time: 5 minutes

2 ounces Pappy Van Winkle bourbon

¾ ounce fresh lemon juice

¾ ounce Demerara syrup (see headnote)

½ ounce crème de pêche

Ice

1 ounce club soda

4 dashes Peychaud's bitters

1 lemon wheel

1. Combine the bourbon, lemon juice, Demerara syrup, and crème de pêche in a cocktail shaker. Add ice; shake for 15 seconds.

2. Strain the mixture into a highball glass and top with the club soda. Garnish with the bitters and lemon wheel and serve.

Peninsula's Gin and Peach Tonic

This recipe comes from Craig Schoen, the man behind the bar program at Peninsula, an Iberian-inspired restaurant in East Nashville. He is a master of the gin and tonic, having been influenced during a trip to Spain by the diversity of gins and the inventive ways bartenders were mixing them up. This one is fantastic, with whole slices of peach perched artfully in a glass. Enjoy it with the Snapper Peach Crudo (page 75).

Makes 1 cocktail

Hands-on time: 5 minutes

Total time: 5 minutes

1½ ounces **Ford's gin**

1 (6.8-ounce) bottle **Fever-Tree Mediterranean tonic water**

4 slices peach

Pea greens or flowers, for garnish

Pour gin into an ice-filled burgundy or Collins glass. Top with tonic water and stir. Garnish with the peach slices and pea greens.

DES

SERT

THE SWEET STUFF

When we were dreaming up The Peach Truck, the word *freedom* kept buzzing in the back of our heads. Could we build something that allowed us to manage our own work/life balance? Jessica was the cheerleader for the idea of pursuing a different path, while Stephen took longer to come around to the idea. When a coffee roaster from Kenya guest spoke at his company—expressing how fulfilled he was pursuing work that allowed him to live on his own terms—Stephen made up his mind.

Here's what we thought: we'd work really, really hard for seven months and then be unafraid of enjoying the fruits of our labor for five. That would be the sweet payoff: putting everything into building something, and having unencumbered time to explore the world. And so we did: we set off on eye-opening adventures to places like Thailand, India, Nepal, Jordan, and Greece. In the course of our travels, we've eaten unforgettable meals in Paris, scootered through the rain forests of Phuket, hung out with fruit vendors in India, and heard stories from Syrian refugees in Jordan. The people we talked to and the cultures to which we've been exposed stay with us to this day.

Even after the arrival of our children, when we could no longer spend months traveling, we are grateful for the time we've been able to spend together as a family in the off-season.

During the height of peach season, that time is admittedly more difficult to come by, but one of our favorite summer rituals is eating peaches after dinner with Florence, Wyatt, and Rainier. In that twilight hour when the kids are starting to fall apart, we head off to the front porch with peaches and napkins in hand. Kids and peaches are like magnets to each other, and trying to control the syrupy chaos is impossible, so Jessica, a self-proclaimed neat freak, decided we'd strip them down to essentially nothing (which is all they've ever wanted anyway) and sit them outside while they squish and throw and nosh on ripe peaches. The albums on our phones every summer are littered with shots of this tradition: naked babies covered head to toe in peach pulp. Then we pull out the hose and spray them as they run squealing through the water. That porch, their sticky smiles, that spray of water—they're our saving graces on a hot day. It's our family's sweet spot.

So we celebrate those moments of freedom—whether it's exploring a city halfway around the world or watching three tiny humans happily smash peaches into their hair. That's what we love about the recipes in this chapter: some are grand and elaborate, while some feel familiar and homey, but all signal celebration. Some tap into the sweet lore of the South—where tea comes with sugar, biscuits come with jelly, and chess pie was created out of pantry staples that preserved easily in an unrefrigerated chest. Many honor our favorite restaurants in Nashville and the pastry chefs and culinary trailblazers who have inspired us as we've embarked on our own path. More than a few recipes remind us of traditions from our own families: Stephen never bites into a cobbler without thinking of his mother, who baked them throughout the Georgia winters with fresh peaches frozen months before. For Jessica, the act of making a pie is the ultimate labor of love, one that she can trace to women from every part of her life who swear by a pie crust recipe or a secret ingredient. Who revel in the sweetness of the everyday.

Peach-Plum Cupcakes
and Buttercream Frosting

Here's why we love a cupcake: it's a small token that brings a touch of joy to anyone upon whom it's bestowed. These are especially flavorful and moist, thanks to a mix of rich spices and irresistibly fluffy peach-plum frosting. The compote can be made up to one week ahead and stored in an airtight container in the fridge.

Makes 16 cupcakes
Hands-on time: 35 minutes
Total time: 1 hour 35 minutes

PEACH-PLUM COMPOTE

1½ cups chopped peaches
(about 2 medium)

1½ cups chopped plums
(about 4 medium)

⅔ cup granulated sugar

1 teaspoon lemon zest

2 teaspoons fresh lemon juice

2 teaspoons cornstarch

¼ teaspoon ground
cardamom

¼ teaspoon ground
cinnamon

Pinch of kosher salt

CUPCAKES

1½ cups all-purpose flour

1 teaspoon baking powder

½ teaspoon kosher salt

½ cup (1 stick) salted butter,
at room temperature

1 cup granulated sugar

1 large egg

2 egg whites

2 teaspoons vanilla bean
paste or extract

¼ cup whole milk

PEACH-PLUM BUTTERCREAM

1 cup (2 sticks) salted butter,
at room temperature

3½ cups powdered sugar

½ teaspoon vanilla bean
paste or extract

1. To make the compote, combine the peaches, plums, granulated sugar, lemon zest, lemon juice, cornstarch, cardamom, cinnamon, and salt in a medium saucepan. Bring to a simmer over medium heat and cook, stirring frequently and mashing occasionally, until the fruit is broken down and the mixture has thickened, about 12 minutes. Transfer to a medium bowl and let cool completely.

2. Preheat the oven to 350°F. Line 16 muffin cups with paper liners.

3. To make the cupcakes, whisk together the flour, baking powder, and salt in a medium bowl. Beat the butter in a large bowl with a handheld mixer on medium speed until fluffy, about 2 minutes. Gradually add the granulated sugar and beat until

light and fluffy, about 2 minutes. Beat in the egg, egg whites, and vanilla. Reduce the speed to low and add the flour mixture, alternating with the milk, beginning and ending with the flour. Set aside ¼ cup of the cooled compote for the buttercream and fold the remaining compote into the batter.

4. Spoon the batter into the prepared muffin cups. Bake for 20 to 25 minutes, until a pick inserted into the center of a cupcake comes out clean. Let cool in the pans for 5 minutes, then transfer to wire racks to cool completely.

5. To make the buttercream, beat the butter in a large bowl with a handheld mixer on medium speed for 2 minutes, or until fluffy. Reduce the speed to low and gradually beat in the powdered sugar. Add the vanilla; increase the speed to medium and beat for 1 minute, or until light and fluffy. Add the reserved ¼ cup compote and stir until combined.

6. Spread the buttercream onto the cupcakes with a spatula. Though best served immediately, these can be stored in an airtight container in the refrigerator for 2 days. Let come to room temperature before eating.

Fresh Peach Milk Shake

Oh my, the joy of a milk shake! As kids, we both had the same rule from our parents when we would eat out: no ordering drinks or desserts. So if you were allowed to order a milk shake, you knew it was a special night. This one is truly decadent, with a rich combination of textures courtesy of the peaches, cookie crumbles, and whipped cream. You can make it into an adult drink by adding one quarter cup of the syrup left over from making Peach Rum Conserve (page 252).

Makes 6½ cups; serves 4
Hands-on time: 5 minutes
Total time: 5 minutes

4 cups sliced peaches (about 4 medium)

2 pints vanilla ice cream, softened

½ cup whole milk

1 teaspoon pure vanilla extract

¼ teaspoon almond extract

Pinch of kosher salt

1 cup sweetened whipped cream

¼ cup crushed almond cookies

1. Combine the peaches, ice cream, milk, vanilla, almond extract, and salt in a blender. Blend for 1 minute, or until thick, smooth, and creamy.

2. Pour the mixture into four glasses. Top each glass evenly with the whipped cream and sprinkle with the crushed cookies.

Peach Pavlova
with Whipped Cream

This pavlova looks far more complicated to make than it is, so whip it up if you're looking to impress people but are feeling short on time. Using superfine sugar is important here, as it easily dissolves into the egg whites and won't ooze or seep from the meringue during baking. Don't have any on hand? Grind granulated sugar in a food processor until very fine. When it comes to assembly, this is definitely a case of more is more. The higher you pile the whipped cream and the more peaches you tumble on top, the more majestic the result.

Serves 8
Hands-on time: 30 minutes
Total time: 5 hours 45 minutes

MERINGUE

3 tablespoons cornstarch

2 cups superfine sugar

8 large egg whites,
   at room temperature

2 teaspoons fresh lemon juice

½ teaspoon pure vanilla
   extract

½ teaspoon kosher salt

PEACHES

3 tablespoons unsalted butter

4 large peaches, pitted and
   each cut into 16 wedges
   (about 6 cups)

1 cinnamon stick

2 tablespoons fresh
   lemon juice

½ cup superfine sugar

½ teaspoon kosher salt

½ teaspoon pure vanilla
   extract

½ cup brandy

1. To make the meringue, preheat the oven to 250°F. Line a large baking sheet with parchment paper.

2. Whisk together the cornstarch and sugar in a medium bowl.

3. Beat together the egg whites, lemon juice, vanilla, and salt with a handheld mixer on medium speed until foamy. Increase the speed to medium-high and gradually add the cornstarch mixture, 1 tablespoon at a time. Beat until stiff, glossy peaks form, about 8 minutes.

4. Spoon the meringue onto the prepared baking sheet and spread it into a roughly 12 x 9-inch rectangle. Bake for 2 hours 15 minutes, or until set and firm. The meringue should lift easily from the parchment when it is ready. Turn the oven off and let the pavlova sit in the oven until cooled completely, at least 3 hours or up to overnight.

5. To make the peaches, melt the butter in a Dutch oven or large deep skillet over medium-high heat. Add the peaches, cinnamon stick, lemon juice, sugar, salt, and vanilla. Remove from the heat and carefully add the brandy. Carefully return the pan to the heat. Cook, stirring frequently, for 5 to 7 minutes, until the peaches are tender and the mixture is syrupy. Remove from the heat.

WHIPPED CREAM

1½ cups heavy cream

¼ cup superfine sugar

1 teaspoon pure vanilla extract

TO ASSEMBLE

2 tablespoons torn fresh lemon balm or mint leaves

6. To assemble the pavlova, beat the cream, sugar, and vanilla with a handheld mixer on high speed until soft peaks form. Spread the whipped cream over the meringue. Remove and discard the cinnamon stick from the peaches. Top the pavlova with the peaches and any juices from the pan, and garnish with the lemon balm. Serve immediately.

Peach and Rhubarb Slab Pie

Are you a crust person? Then this dessert—with a high crust-to-filling ratio—is for you. We love rhubarb, and the way supersweet peaches balance its tart profile. Best of all, you can make it in summer with fresh fruit, or substitute frozen for a cold-weather indulgence. Beautifully rustic, this pie is also easy to travel with, so bring it along to your next summer cookout or wintry dinner party.

Makes one 15 x 10-inch pie; serves 8

Hands-on time: 15 minutes

Total time: 2 hours

1 recipe Millie's Crust (page 223)

All-purpose flour, for dusting

½ cup plus 1 tablespoon granulated sugar

⅓ cup packed light brown sugar

Pinch of kosher salt

¼ cup cornstarch

1 pound rhubarb, sliced (about 3 cups)

1 pound peaches, pitted and sliced (about 3 cups)

1 teaspoon vanilla bean paste

1 large egg

1. Preheat the oven to 400°F. Line a baking sheet with parchment paper.

2. Roll out one dough disk on a lightly floured surface to a 17 x 12-inch rectangle. Place the dough in a 15 x 10-inch jelly-roll pan, pressing it into the corners to fit. Roll out the other dough disk to a 17 x 12-inch rectangle. Place it on the prepared baking sheet. Chill the dough while preparing the filling.

3. Whisk together the ½ cup granulated sugar, the brown sugar, salt, and cornstarch in a medium bowl. Add the rhubarb, peaches, and vanilla and stir until well combined. Spoon the filling over the dough in the jelly-roll pan, spreading it so the fruit is in single layer. Top the filling with the rolled-out dough from the baking sheet. Pinch and crimp the edges to seal.

4. Whisk together the egg and 1 tablespoon water in a small bowl. Brush the top crust with the egg wash; sprinkle with the 1 tablespoon granulated sugar. Cut slits in the top to vent steam. Bake for 40 to 45 minutes, until golden brown. Let the pie cool for 1 hour before serving.

Skillet Peach Blueberry Cobbler

Cobbler is the way to Stephen Rose's heart. To him, the salty, sweet, chewy, crunchy perfection in a cast-iron skillet means home, family, and comfort. Bursting with berry and peach flavor in every bite, this recipe brings him right back to his childhood kitchen in Fort Valley. Feel free to swap out the blueberries for raspberries or blackberries.

Serves 6 to 8
Hands-on time: 10 minutes
Total time: 1 hour

1 cup all-purpose flour

1 cup granulated sugar

2 teaspoons baking powder

½ teaspoon kosher salt

1 cup whole milk

1 teaspoon vanilla bean paste

1 teaspoon lemon zest

2 tablespoons fresh lemon juice

½ cup (1 stick) unsalted butter

1 cup blueberries

1½ cups sliced peaches (about 2 medium)

2 tablespoons turbinado sugar

Vanilla ice cream, for serving

1. Preheat the oven to 350°F. Place a 10-inch cast-iron skillet in the oven while it preheats.

2. Whisk together the flour, granulated sugar, baking powder, and salt in a medium bowl. Whisk together the milk, vanilla, lemon zest, and lemon juice in another bowl. Add the milk mixture to the flour mixture and stir until just combined.

3. Place the butter in the hot cast-iron skillet in the oven and heat until the butter melts. Carefully add the batter to the skillet. Scatter the blueberries and peaches over the top. Sprinkle with the turbinado sugar. Bake for 50 minutes, or until golden brown. Serve warm or at room temperature, with ice cream.

Peach Pie

As the story goes, Jessica's dear aunt Sue was a newlywed trying to impress guests when she made a pie with a crust so notoriously burnt that it is still the lore of her family today. Sue went to her mother, Millie, begging for help; and that was when she learned about the secret ingredient to making a pie crust sing: apple cider vinegar. In a pie, it tenderizes the crust, making it flaky and easier to work with; in life, Jessica's family subscribes to the belief that it is the antidote to any ailment (Stephen remains skeptical).

Regardless of where you fall on the magical properties of apple cider vinegar, we think you'll find this crust to be a standout—buttery and an excellent complement to summer peaches, minimally flavored with lemon and vanilla to let them shine.

Serves 8
Hands-on time: 20 minutes
Total time: 5 hours 25 minutes

MILLIE'S CRUST

3 cups all-purpose flour, plus more for dusting

1 tablespoon sugar

½ teaspoon salt

1¼ cups cubed cold vegetable shortening

5 tablespoons ice water

1 tablespoon apple cider vinegar

1 large egg

FILLING

4 pounds peaches, pitted and sliced (about 12 cups)

½ cup plus 1 tablespoon sugar

¼ cup cornstarch

Pinch of kosher salt

2 tablespoons fresh lemon juice

1 teaspoon vanilla bean paste or pure vanilla extract

1 large egg

1. To make the crust, sift together the flour, sugar, and salt into a medium bowl. Cut in the shortening with a pastry blender until the mixture resembles large peas. Whisk together the ice water, vinegar, and egg in a small bowl. Add the egg mixture to the flour mixture and stir with a fork until just combined. Divide the dough in half; flatten each half into a disk and wrap in plastic wrap. Chill for 2 hours or up to overnight.

2. Preheat the oven to 425°F. Line a baking sheet with parchment paper.

3. Roll out one dough disk on a lightly floured surface to a round about ¼ inch thick. Fit the dough into a 9-inch pie plate. Roll out the other dough disk to a round about ¼ inch thick. Place the round of dough on the prepared baking sheet. Cut it into 2½-inch-wide strips. Chill the dough while preparing the filling.

4. To make the filling, combine the peaches, the ½ cup sugar, the cornstarch, salt, lemon juice, and vanilla in a large bowl.

5. Spoon the filling into the dough-lined pie plate. Arrange the pastry strips on the top of the pie in a lattice. Fold the edges under and crimp. Beat the egg and 1 tablespoon water together in a small bowl. Brush the egg wash lightly over the top crust. Sprinkle with the 1 tablespoon sugar.

6. Line a baking sheet with aluminum foil and place it on the bottom rack of the oven (this is to catch any filling that bubbles over). Bake the pie on the center rack for 15 minutes. Reduce the oven temperature to 375°F and bake for 40 to 50 minutes more, until golden brown and bubbling, shielding the pie with a sheet of foil after 20 minutes if the crust is getting too brown. Let cool completely on a wire rack, about 2 hours, before slicing and serving.

Peach Sorbet

For parents, summer is all about trying to create kid-friendly dishes that take advantage of what's in season. Peach sorbet checks off all the boxes: a warm-weather treat that's super easy to whip up and makes kids giddy with excitement. Every time we watch our children's anticipatory faces as we lift a tray of sorbet out of the freezer, we go back to feeling like kids ourselves. What is better, in the summer, than knowing a frozen dessert is coming your way?

Use peaches that are as soft as possible; they'll be the best for flavor and texture. Before serving, let the sorbet soften at room temperature for fifteen minutes, or use a scoop that's been dipped in hot water.

Serves 10

Hands-on time: 5 minutes

Total time: 5 minutes, plus churning and overnight freezing time

2½ pounds very ripe peaches, pitted and coarsely chopped

¾ cup plus 2 tablespoons sugar

2 tablespoons fresh lemon juice

Pinch of kosher salt

1. Combine the peaches, sugar, lemon juice, and salt in a food processor; process until smooth.

2. Pour the mixture into an ice cream machine. Process according to the manufacturer's instructions. Transfer to a freezer-safe container and place a piece of parchment paper directly on the surface of the sorbet. Wrap in plastic wrap and freeze for 4 hours or up to overnight before serving. The sorbet will keep in the freezer for up to 1 week.

Fried Peach Pies

These pies always remind Stephen of his feisty grandmother. One afternoon, when he was sixteen and had just gotten his license, he drove her to McDonald's for their notorious fried pie deal: two hot apple pies for ninety-nine cents. Having served as a dutiful grandson, Stephen assumed one of the pies in the papery McDonald's bag was for him . . . until he reached in and his grandmother shooed away his hand! Both warm pies, it turns out, were for her. Now any fried pie—even these peach ones, curved into little half-moons—makes him think of his grandmother. He loved her, but boy, was she not letting him anywhere near her pies.

The filling and the pie dough for these can be made a day ahead and stored in the refrigerator, and the actual pies can be filled and shaped a few hours before frying. Wrap them tightly with plastic wrap and refrigerate until ready to fry.

Makes 12 hand pies
Hands-on time: 55 minutes
Total time: 2 hours 55 minutes

FILLING

2 medium peaches, peeled (see page 245), pitted, and sliced (about 2 cups)

1 tablespoon fresh lemon juice

½ cup granulated sugar

½ teaspoon ground cardamom

1 tablespoon cornstarch

1 tablespoon cold salted butter

CRUST

5 cups all-purpose flour, plus more for dusting

2 teaspoons kosher salt

½ cup plus 2 tablespoons cubed cold shortening

6 tablespoons (¾ stick) cold unsalted butter, cubed

10 to 16 tablespoons ice water

Vegetable oil, for frying

Powdered sugar, for dusting

1. To make the filling, place the peach slices in a medium saucepan. Add the lemon juice, granulated sugar, and cardamom. Bring to a boil over medium-high heat. Reduce the heat to maintain a simmer, cover, and cook for 5 minutes. Break up the peaches slightly with a spoon. Mix the cornstarch with 1 tablespoon water in a small bowl and pour the mixture into the pan with the peach mixture. Bring to a boil and cook until thickened, about 30 seconds. Remove from the heat and stir in the butter until it has melted. Cover and chill for 2 hours or until cold.

(recipe continues)

2. To make the crust, place the flour and salt in a food processor and pulse a few times to combine. Add the shortening and butter; pulse eight times, or until the mixture resembles large peas. Add 10 tablespoons of the ice water and pulse eight times, or until the mixture starts to come together, adding the additional water as necessary, 1 tablespoon at a time. Squeeze a small amount of the dough in your fist; if it holds together, it is ready. If it crumbles apart, add more water. Divide the dough in half and form each half into a disk. Wrap in plastic wrap and chill for 1 hour.

3. To make the pies, line two baking sheets with parchment paper. Roll out one dough disk on a lightly floured surface to ⅛-inch thickness. Using a round cutter, cut out six 5-inch rounds. Place the rounds of dough on one of the prepared baking sheets and refrigerate. Repeat with the second dough disk.

4. Place a heaping tablespoon of the chilled filling in the center of each dough round. Do not overfill. You will want a minimum of 1 inch of exposed dough around the edges. Using a brush or your finger, wet half of the outer edge of the circle with water to help the dough seal. Carefully fold the dough in half to make a half-moon shape, pressing the edges to seal. Use the tines of a fork to crimp and secure the edges. Refrigerate the hand pies while heating the oil.

5. Fill a Dutch oven or deep skillet with vegetable oil to a depth of 2 inches. Heat the oil over medium heat to 350°F. Line a baking sheet with paper towels and set it nearby. Carefully place 3 or 4 pies at a time in the hot oil and fry until deep golden brown, about 6 minutes, turning as necessary to ensure even browning. Drain the hand pies on the paper towels and dust with powdered sugar. Serve the same day, warm or at room temperature.

Pearson Farm Bourbon Peach Bread Pudding

This is a goodie from our friends at Pearson Farm, a simple classic that we've enjoyed frequently when we're down there; the peach bourbon gives it a warm and welcome kick. Now that we make it ourselves, we've learned it's just as good for breakfast the next day with a cup of strong coffee.

Use challah or any bread that's a few days past its prime. Chilling the bread mixture for an hour before baking helps the bread absorb the liquid, resulting in better texture and flavor. The sauce can be made a day or two ahead and refrigerated.

Serves 9
Hands-on time: 15 minutes
Total time: 2 hours 5 minutes

PUDDING

1¼ cups 1% milk

1 (12-ounce) can evaporated skim milk

¾ cup packed brown sugar

¼ cup bourbon

1 tablespoon pure vanilla extract

¼ teaspoon freshly grated nutmeg

¼ teaspoon ground cinnamon

3 large eggs, lightly beaten

2½ cups chopped peeled (see page 245) peaches (about 3 medium)

8 cups (1-inch cubes) challah or other bread

Canola oil, for greasing

SAUCE

⅓ cup granulated sugar

2 tablespoons salted butter

1 cup 1% milk

1 tablespoon cornstarch

2 tablespoons white chocolate chips

1 teaspoon pure vanilla extract

1. To make the pudding, whisk together the 1% milk, evaporated milk, brown sugar, bourbon, vanilla, nutmeg, cinnamon, and eggs in a large bowl. Add the peaches and bread and toss to combine. Cover and chill for 1 hour.

2. Preheat the oven to 350°F. Lightly oil an 11 x 8-inch baking dish.

3. Spoon the bread mixture into the prepared baking dish. Bake for 50 minutes, or until golden brown and set in the center.

4. To make the sauce, melt the granulated sugar and butter in a medium saucepan over medium heat.

(recipe continues)

5. In a medium bowl, whisk together the milk and cornstarch. Add the milk mixture to the saucepan with the sugar mixture and bring to a boil over medium-high heat. Reduce the heat to medium-low, stir in the white chocolate and vanilla, and cook until the sauce is smooth and thickened, 2 to 3 minutes.

6. Spoon out a generous amount and drizzle some of the sauce over each serving.

Josephine's Ricotta Cake
with Elderflower Peaches

Here's a recipe we'll guarantee you'll revisit again and again. French Culinary Institute alumna Kayla May is the pastry chef at Josephine, the charming 12 South restaurant serving thoughtful unfussy American cuisine. She'll tell you she likes to serve this custardlike cake family style, baked in a casserole, so it can be scooped right out of the pan. It's balanced, refreshing, and perfect for a summer get-together.

Serves 8 to 10

Hands-on time: 32 minutes

Total time: 2 hours 17 minutes plus overnight

WHIPPED WHITE CHOCOLATE

2 cups heavy cream, plus more if needed

1 teaspoon vanilla bean paste

7 ounces white chocolate, chopped (1⅓ cups)

¼ teaspoon salt

PEACH PUREE

8 medium peaches

½ cup sugar

2 tablespoons fresh lime juice

2 tablespoons gin

¼ cup St-Germain elderflower liqueur

RICOTTA CAKE

1⅓ cups ricotta cheese

1 cup sugar

⅓ cup cornstarch

½ teaspoon salt

1 teaspoon vanilla bean paste

½ teaspoon lemon zest

2 tablespoons fresh lemon juice

8 large egg yolks

7 large egg whites, at room temperature

1. To make the whipped white chocolate, combine the cream and vanilla in a medium saucepan and bring to a boil over medium-high heat. Put the white chocolate in a heatproof medium bowl and pour the hot cream over the top; let sit for 1 minute. Add the salt and whisk until smooth. Cover, let cool, and refrigerate overnight.

(recipe continues)

2.   Beat the white chocolate mixture with a handheld mixer on medium-high speed for 1 minute, or until thickened, adding more cream if necessary for a softer consistency. Cover and chill for up to 2 hours until ready to use.

3.   To make the peach puree, peel (see page 244), pit, and coarsely chop 5 of the peaches. Puree in a blender or food processor until smooth.

4.   In a medium saucepan, combine the peach puree, sugar, and lime juice. Cook over medium heat, stirring until the sugar has dissolved. Remove from the heat; stir in the gin and elderflower liqueur.

5.   Pit and slice the remaining 3 peaches, place them in the warm puree, and let cool. (The peach puree can be made a day ahead and refrigerated overnight—it only gets better with time.)

6.   To make the ricotta cake, preheat the oven to 325°F. Lightly coat a 13 x 9-inch baking dish with nonstick cooking spray.

7.   In a large bowl, combine the ricotta, ½ cup of the sugar, the cornstarch, salt, vanilla, lemon zest, and lemon juice and mix until combined. Whisk in the egg yolks.

8.   In a clean bowl, beat the egg whites with a handheld mixer on medium-high speed until foamy. Slowly add the remaining ½ cup sugar and whip until medium peaks form.

9.   Gently fold the beaten egg whites into the ricotta mixture, making sure there are no streaks of white left.

10. Pour the batter into the prepared baking dish. Bake until golden around the edges and set in the middle, 40 to 45 minutes. Let the cake cool completely in the pan on a wire rack. The cake will double in height while baking and then settle back down once cool.

11. Scoop the cake into individual serving bowls. Finish each serving with a generous dollop of whipped white chocolate and top with the marinated peaches and their juices.

Lemon Peach Pound Cake

Warning: If you make this recipe, you might accidentally eat the entire loaf (we speak from experience). It was given to us courtesy of Lisa Donovan, a pastry chef and writer who was baking at Husk when we started delivering our peaches in the early days. Stephen quickly fell into a routine of looking forward to seeing her every week, getting a big hug, and hearing about her plans for whatever variety we had in the truck. We think back on it as a special time, when we were both coming up in Nashville, and charting uncertain and exciting paths. To us, she's integral to the soul of the city; one of those rare talents who makes Nashville what it is.

Her pound cake—airy, lemony, and moist—uses cornmeal as a base. That quintessentially Southern grain pairs beautifully with the lemon zest and peaches (chop them finely for optimal distribution throughout the loaf).

Serves 16

Hands-on time: 1 hour 15 minutes

Total time: 2 hours 15 minutes

1 cup (2 sticks) unsalted butter, at room temperature, plus more for the pans

1¾ cups all-purpose flour, plus more for the pans

½ cup coarse yellow cornmeal (preferably Anson Mills Sweet Appalachian)

2 teaspoons baking powder

1½ teaspoons salt

½ cup buttermilk

¼ cup whole milk

1 teaspoon vanilla bean paste or extract

1½ cups granulated sugar

2 tablespoons lemon zest

4 large eggs, at room temperature

2 cups chopped peaches (about 2 medium)

2 cups powdered sugar, plus more if needed

¼ cup fresh lemon juice, plus more if needed

1. Preheat the oven to 350°F. Grease two 8 x 4-inch loaf pans with butter, dust them with flour, and tap out any excess (or use a good-quality baker's spray).

2. Whisk together the flour, cornmeal, baking powder, and salt in a large bowl. Set aside.

3. Combine the buttermilk and milk in a small bowl. Whisk in the vanilla. Set aside.

(recipe continues)

4. Cream the butter and granulated sugar in a large bowl using a handheld mixer on medium speed until fluffy, about 3 minutes. Add the lemon zest. Beat until combined. Add the eggs one at a time, beating until each egg is well incorporated before adding the next. Beat until the mixture is thoroughly combined.

5. Add the flour mixture to the butter mixture in three additions, alternating with the milk mixture, beginning and ending with the flour mixture; stop to scrape down the sides of the bowl often. Beat the batter for a final 30 to 60 seconds, until thoroughly combined. Fold in the peaches.

6. Pour the batter evenly into the prepared pans and bake for 50 minutes to 1 hour, until a pick inserted into the center of the cake comes out clean. Let cool in the pans on a wire rack for 1 hour. Remove the cakes from the pans.

7. Whisk together the powdered sugar and lemon juice in a small bowl to make a glaze, adding more sugar and/or juice as needed to adjust the consistency.

8. Pour the glaze over the top of the cake and let set before slicing and serving.

Buttermilk Panna Cotta

with Macerated Peaches

Pastry chef Rebekah Turshen from City House has used her genius to create what little kids might call fancy Jell-O and adults would call heaven. In this amazing dessert, the natural yellow hue comes through, above the rich, creamy white layer below, making the whole thing look as classic as lemon meringue pie. Grab your cookie and dip—and be sure to get a heap of the macerated peaches. Layer that cookie right, and the rest will follow.

Heat the gelatin gently—never let it boil or simmer. You can make the cookie dough up to two months ahead and freeze it, and the panna cotta can be made a day ahead.

Serves 8

Hands-on time: 1 hour 5 minutes

Total time: 5 hours 45 minutes

SHORTBREAD

¾ cup unsalted butter, at room temperature

⅔ cup plus 1 tablespoon sugar

1¼ cups unbleached all-purpose flour

6 tablespoons stone-ground cornmeal

1 teaspoon kosher salt

PANNA COTTA

2¼ teaspoons unflavored gelatin

2 cups heavy cream

½ cup sugar

1⅔ cups buttermilk

½ teaspoon kosher salt

1. To make the shortbread, beat the butter and the ⅔ cup sugar with a handheld mixer at medium speed until light and fluffy, scraping down the sides of the bowl as needed. Whisk together the flour, cornmeal, and salt. Add to the butter mixture on low speed, beating until just combined. Divide the dough into 2 (6 x 1½-inch) logs. Wrap the logs in plastic wrap and freeze for 2 hours or until firm.

2. Preheat oven to 350°F. Line two baking sheets with parchment paper. Slice the dough into ¼-inch-thick rounds and place them on the prepared baking sheets. Sprinkle the cookies with the 1 tablespoon sugar and a pinch of salt. Bake the cookies for 12 to 15 minutes, or until lightly golden.

3. To make the panna cotta, sprinkle the gelatin over ¼ cup cold water in a small saucepan. Let stand for 5 minutes. Heat 1 cup of the cream and the sugar in a small saucepan until warm (do not boil). Gently heat the gelatin over low heat until it dissolves. Add the warm cream to the gelatin mixture, whisking well. Whisk in the remaining 1 cup cream, the buttermilk, and salt.

4. Pour the mixture into eight shallow bowls or large ramekins. Refrigerate for 2 hours or until set.

MACERATED PEACHES

**6 cups peeled (see page 245)
and coarsely torn peaches
(about 6 medium)**

1⅓ cups sugar

1 lemon zested and juiced

1 teaspoon cider vinegar

PEACH JELLY

**2 teaspoons unflavored
gelatin**

5. To macerate the peaches, combine the peaches, sugar, lemon zest, lemon juice, and vinegar in a medium bowl. Let stand for 30 minutes. Strain off 2 cups of the liquid to use for the peach jelly.

6. To make the peach jelly, sprinkle the gelatin over 3 tablespoons cold water in a small skillet. Heat ½ cup of the reserved peach juice until warm (do not boil). Gently heat the gelatin over low heat until the gelatin dissolves. Add the warm peach juice and remaining cold peach juice to the gelatin mixture. Pour the mixture evenly over the set custards. Refrigerate until the jelly is set, about 45 minutes.

7. Serve the custards with the macerated peaches and shortbread cookies.

Peach Tarte Tatins

This simple yet impressive dessert is great for entertaining: each guest gets his or her own ramekin, bubbling with peaches, butter, and cinnamon. Use half a peach here and don't be shy—you'll need it to balance the richness of the pastry. We prefer Dufour puff pastry for its flavor, which you can find in the freezer section of most select grocery stores.

Makes 6 tarts
Hands-on time: 20 minutes
Total time: 1 hour 5 minutes

3 tablespoons salted butter, at room temperature

1 (14-ounce) package frozen puff pastry, thawed

All-purpose flour, for dusting

¾ cup sugar

3 medium peaches, halved and pitted

TOPPING

2 tablespoons salted butter, melted

2 tablespoons sugar

½ teaspoon ground cinnamon

Crème fraîche, whipped cream, or ice cream, for serving

1. Preheat the oven to 375°F. Butter six 10-ounce ramekins.

2. Roll out the puff pastry on a lightly floured surface. Using a ramekin as a template, cut out 6 rounds. Refrigerate the pastry rounds while preparing the caramel.

3. Combine the sugar and 2 tablespoon water in a small saucepan and cook over medium heat, swirling the pan occasionally (do not stir), until the mixture turns an amber color. Immediately divide the caramel evenly among the prepared ramekins.

4. Place one peach half, cut side down, on top of the caramel in each ramekin. Place a pastry round over each peach, tucking the edges around the fruit.

5. To make the topping, brush the tops of each pastry with the melted butter. Combine the sugar and cinnamon in a small bowl; sprinkle evenly over the tops of each pastry. Bake for 30 to 40 minutes, until the pastry is golden brown. Let the pastries cool in the ramekins for 5 minutes, then immediately invert each onto an individual serving plate.

6. Drizzle any caramel remaining in the ramekin over the top of the tarte tatin. Serve warm, with crème fraîche, whipped cream, or ice cream.

Jeni's Cold-Poached Peaches

with Raspberries and Peach Buttermilk Ice Cream

We first sat down to dinner with Jeni Britton Bauer of Jeni's Splendid Ice Creams at a City House Sunday Supper in 2013. As entrepreneurs testing the waters with a product and business idea ourselves, we were fascinated to hear about how she got into making ice cream, from her early days at the North Market in Columbus, Ohio, to the beloved nationwide e-commerce, grocery, and brick-and-mortar business she runs now. We told her about what we were trying to do with our peaches and our goal of introducing them throughout Nashville, the South, and the country. The next day, we received a call asking if we'd like to work together. Since that call, Jeni's Splendid Ice Creams has churned our peaches into a flavor every summer, and we're honored to be a part of what she's doing. We love that through her ice cream, our peaches make it to Los Angeles, Chicago, Charlotte, and beyond.

Okay, on to the ice cream. Jeni developed a method for cold-poaching peaches to preserve a perfectly ripe peach for about three days. The results are tender and fragrant, just right for an irresistible—and couldn't-be-prettier—peach melba that will ruin you for anyone else's.

Serves 4

Hands-on time: 15 minutes

Total time: 15 hours 15 minutes

1 cup sugar

1 lemon, juiced (about 3 tablespoons)

½ cup peach schnapps

4 medium peaches

1. In a small saucepan, bring 1 cup water to a boil. Add the sugar and lemon juice and whisk until the sugar has completely dissolved. Add the schnapps and refrigerate until cold (about 3 hours).

2. Wash the peaches under running water. If desired, peel the peaches with a soft skin peeler or a small knife. Halve and pit the peaches. Discard the pit and any remaining fruit stem.

3. Place the peach halves in the sugar syrup, top with a salad plate to submerge the fruit, and let sit overnight (at least 12 hours).

(recipe continues)

PEACH BUTTERMILK ICE CREAM

2¼ medium peaches, peeled (see page 245), pitted, and chopped

1 cup whole milk

2 tablespoons cornstarch

2 ounces cream cheese, at room temperature

⅛ teaspoon fine sea salt

1¼ cups heavy cream

⅔ cup sugar

2 tablespoons light corn syrup

½ cup buttermilk

1 pint raspberries, rinsed

¼ cup crumbled amaretti cookies, or any cookie you prefer

4. To make the ice cream, puree the peaches in a food processor. Set aside ½ cup of the pureed peaches; refrigerate the rest of the puree for another use.

5. Mix about 2 tablespoons of the milk with the cornstarch in a small bowl to make a smooth slurry. Whisk the cream cheese and salt in a medium bowl until smooth. Fill a large bowl with ice and water and set it aside nearby.

6. Combine the remaining milk, the heavy cream, sugar, and corn syrup in a 4-quart saucepan, bringing the mixture to a rolling boil over medium-high heat, and cook for 4 minutes. Remove from the heat and gradually whisk in the cornstarch slurry. Bring the mixture back to a boil over medium-high heat and cook, stirring with a heatproof spatula, until slightly thickened, about 1 minute. Remove from the heat.

7. Gradually whisk the hot milk mixture into the cream cheese until smooth. Add the reserved peach puree and the buttermilk and blend well. Pour the mixture into a 1-gallon zip-top freezer bag, seal it, and submerge it in the ice bath. Let stand, adding more ice as necessary, until cold, about 30 minutes.

8. Pour the ice cream base into an ice cream maker and churn according to the manufacturer's instructions until thick and creamy. Pack the ice cream into an airtight freezer-safe storage container, press a sheet of parchment paper directly against the surface, and cover with the airtight lid. Freeze in the coldest part of your freezer until firm, at least 4 hours.

9. To assemble the dessert, remove the peaches from the syrup and plate them, reserving the syrup. Toss the raspberries with the reserved peach syrup, breaking them lightly with a fork. Spoon over the peaches and top with the crushed cookies. Serve with the ice cream.

HOW TO BLANCH
AND PEEL A PEACH

The easiest way to blanch and peel them for baking, canning, or freezing.

1. Fill a pot with enough water to cover the peaches and bring to a boil. Fill a large bowl with ice and water and set it nearby.

2. Make a small X in the skin on the bottom of each peach, trying not to cut into the flesh. Drop the peaches into the boiling water and cook for 30 seconds.

3. Promptly remove the peaches with a slotted spoon or tongs and place them in the bowl of ice water. Let cool.

4. Once they have cooled, remove the peaches from the ice water, and, starting at the corners of the X, gently peel the skin.

PANTRY

YOUR FUTURE SELF
THANKS YOU

Like many people, we put effort into living in the present, whether it's spending time with our kids, with each other, or experiencing the challenges and hard-won victories of running a business. This chapter of recipes, however, is all about the future. It's sad to see it go, but there's a lot of joy to each peach season; here, you'll find creative ways to extend its sweetness and bounty throughout the year.

The ritual of "putting up" fruit is one Jessica observed from childhood. To this day, her mother spends weekends in the summer transforming buckets of fresh raspberries and blackberries into jams. It's long, hard work, but when she sends little jars of conserve to friends and family during the holiday season and they open a jar and are greeted by the lush aroma of warmer months, it truly feels like a precious gift.

These days, we try to make peach season last as long as possible with many of the techniques you'll find in this chapter. We surprised even ourselves by how many methods we felt we had to include—so many recipes for a section about a pantry? But the truth is, we've seen firsthand the brightness a jar or a sauce or a spread of preserved peaches can bring to a meal in the middle of winter. Every off-season, we live for the photos people send us of what they're doing with peaches they bought from us so many months ago. It's especially fun to hear from members of our young staff. Canning has really made a comeback among people in their twenties, and we're always blown away by how many people are enthusiastically putting up their peaches from The Peach Truck.

We are fond of the phrase, "Your future self thanks you," because we've found it to be overwhelmingly true, whether it comes to saving money, getting in a half hour of exercise, planting peach trees, or abstaining from one more bourbon late in the night. It's definitely true when it comes to preserving peaches. Bring out your Peach Hot Sauce (page 271) at a festive holiday gathering in December, or a peach chutney or jam to go alongside a cheese plate on a brittle night in February, and watch people say, "What is this? How did you get it? What did you do?"

So try out these recipes, and enjoy peaches all year long—we think you'll thank us later. Your future self will thank you, too.

Peach Rum Conserve

Prepared so that small pieces of the peach remain beautifully intact, this conserve can be muddled into cocktails, drizzled over ice cream, or blended into milk shakes. We highly recommend making a double batch—it will be gone before you know it.

Makes 2¼ cups
Hands-on time: 10 minutes
Total time: 2 hours 10 minutes, plus cooling time

1 pound peaches, pitted and coarsely chopped (about 3 medium)

¾ cup sugar

1 strip lemon peel (peeled with a vegetable peeler)

2 tablespoons fresh lemon juice

⅓ cup dark rum

1 cinnamon stick

Pinch of kosher salt

1 teaspoon cornstarch

⅛ teaspoon vanilla bean paste

1. Combine the peaches, sugar, lemon peel, lemon juice, rum, cinnamon stick, and salt in a medium saucepan. Cover and let stand at room temperature for 2 hours.

2. Set the pot over medium heat and bring to a simmer. Cook for 3 minutes, or until the peaches are just tender. Remove the peaches from the liquid, reserving the cooking liquid in the pot.

3. Whisk 1 tablespoon of the cooking liquid into the cornstarch in a small bowl until blended. Bring the remaining liquid to a simmer over medium heat and cook for 5 minutes, or until the liquid has reduced to ½ cup. Whisk the cornstarch mixture into the liquid in the saucepan and stir until the mixture comes back to a simmer and has thickened slightly. Remove from the heat. Remove and discard the lemon peel and cinnamon stick. Stir in the vanilla.

4. Pour the syrup over the peaches. Let cool. Store, covered, in the refrigerator for up to 2 weeks.

The Peach Truck Freezer Jam

This jam has high-quality ingredients, but is great for every day—you don't have to tuck it away in a corner and save it for special occasions. It's also wonderfully easy to make: no spattering of hot fruit, no canning—just a simple way to preserve the taste of summer.

Using very ripe peaches is important to ensure the smooth texture and optimal flavor of the jam. Thaw the jam in the refrigerator and keep it refrigerated after thawing. It will keep in the freezer for up to a year, and the refrigerator for up to three weeks.

Makes five ½-pint jars

Hands-on time: 12 minutes

Total time: 1 hour 12 minutes, plus overnight freezing time

2 pounds peaches, peeled (see page 245), pitted, and sliced (about 3½ cups)

1½ cups sugar

2 tablespoons fresh lemon juice

1 (1¾-ounce) package less-sugar/no-sugar-needed pectin

1. Pulse the peaches in a food processor until coarsely chopped or mash them with a potato masher, leaving some small chunks. Stir in the sugar and lemon juice.

2. Combine ½ cup water and the pectin in a small saucepan. Bring to a rolling boil, whisking continuously and cook, for 1 minute. Pour over the peach mixture and stir for 1 minute, or until well combined and beginning to thicken.

3. Spoon the peach mixture into five clean ½-pint jars, leaving ½ inch of headspace. Place the tops loosely on the jars. Let stand at room temperature for 1 hour. Place in the freezer. Tighten the lids once the jam is frozen.

Peach Applesauce

Our favorite way to mix up a standard staple, this is delicious on its own or served alongside crispy potato pancakes or brioche French toast. It's also fun and easy enough to make with kids, especially if, like our brood, they go through jars of applesauce at a record clip. Granny Smith apples contribute a nice, tart flavor, but any variety will do.

Makes 5 cups
Hands-on time: 40 minutes
Total time: 40 minutes

2 pounds peaches, peeled (see page 245), pitted, and chopped

2 pounds apples, peeled, cored, and chopped

¾ cup maple syrup

¼ cup fresh lemon juice

3 (¼-inch-thick) slices fresh ginger, peeled and chopped

1 cinnamon stick

Pinch of kosher salt

1. Combine the peaches, apples, maple syrup, lemon juice, ginger, cinnamon stick, salt, and 1 cup water in a large Dutch oven or stockpot. Cover and bring to a boil over medium-high heat. Uncover, reduce the heat to medium, and simmer, stirring occasionally, for 30 minutes. Remove and discard the cinnamon stick.

2. Mash the fruit mixture with a potato masher, blend directly in the pot with an immersion blender, or transfer to a food processor and process to the desired consistency. Let cool. Store in airtight containers in the refrigerator for up to 2 weeks or in the freezer for up to 2 months.

Peach Bourbon BBQ Sauce

Sweet but with a little bite, like some of our favorite people, this barbecue sauce always inspires guests to ask us where we bought it, and we *love* telling them we didn't buy it anywhere. The sauce will fill your kitchen with the most ridiculously appetizing aroma as it cooks—just make sure you pay close attention as you're stirring it so it doesn't burn.

Makes 4¼ cups
Hands-on time: 55 minutes
Total time: 55 minutes

3 or 4 medium peaches, pitted and cut into large cubes

2 tablespoons vegetable oil

2½ cups finely chopped sweet onions

3 garlic cloves, minced

1½ cups lightly packed brown sugar

½ cup apple cider vinegar

¾ cup bourbon

¼ cup Worcestershire sauce

½ teaspoon red pepper flakes

3 tablespoons prepared mustard

Pinch of kosher salt

1. Puree the peaches in a food processor until smooth. You should have 3 cups. Set aside.

2. Heat a Dutch oven or large saucepan over medium-low heat. Heat the vegetable oil, then add the onions and garlic. Cover and cook, stirring occasionally, for 10 minutes. Remove from the heat. Stir in the peach puree, brown sugar, vinegar, bourbon, Worcestershire, and red pepper flakes. Carefully return the pot to the heat and bring the mixture to a boil. Reduce the heat to low and simmer, uncovered, stirring occasionally, for 30 to 40 minutes, until thick. Remove from the heat.

3. Stir in the mustard and salt. Let cool, then transfer to an airtight container. If you're making this ahead, transfer it to a nonreactive container and refrigerate for up to 1 month. The sauce will also keep in the freezer for up to 1 year.

Peach Butter

By its name alone, you know that this recipe combines two iconic ingredients into one irresistible hybrid. We couldn't help giving you two versions. Slather the sweet one onto a biscuit or a waffle, and use the savory for melting on steak, fish, a baked potato, or a simple pasta. Both will keep in the fridge, tightly wrapped, for up to one week.

SWEET PEACH BUTTER

Makes about ¾ cup • Hands-on time: 5 minutes • Total time: 2 hours 5 minutes

½ cup (1 stick) salted butter, at room temperature

¼ cup finely chopped peaches (about 1 small)

2 tablespoons light brown sugar

½ teaspoon orange zest

2 teaspoons fresh orange juice

Combine all the ingredients in a medium bowl. Spoon the butter onto the center of a piece of plastic wrap. Shape it into a log and wrap tightly in the plastic wrap. Chill for at least 2 hours.

SAVORY PEACH BUTTER

Makes about ¾ cup • Hands-on time: 5 minutes • Total time: 2 hours 5 minutes

½ cup (1 stick) salted butter, at room temperature

¼ cup finely chopped peaches (about 1 small)

2 teaspoons chopped fresh thyme leaves

1 tablespoon minced shallot

½ teaspoon lemon zest

2 teaspoons fresh lemon juice

⅛ teaspoon ground red pepper

⅛ teaspoon paprika

Combine all the ingredients in a medium bowl. Spoon the butter onto the center of a piece of plastic wrap. Shape it into a log and wrap tightly in the plastic wrap. Chill for at least 2 hours.

Peach Chutney

We're believers that everyone needs a chutney in their pantry; it's a highly versatile condiment that can be served with chicken, fish, or lamb as easily as it can be added to an omelet, a platter of grilled vegetables, or a beautiful cheese plate (see page 37). The irresistible mix of sweet and hot (to make it hotter, just add more chile seeds) also adds a real "ta-da!" effect to any dish.

Makes 3 cups
Hands-on time: 30 minutes
Total time: 30 minutes, plus cooling time

1 tablespoon vegetable oil

1 small Fresno chile or jalapeño, seeded and chopped (about 1 tablespoon)

¾ cup chopped red onion

½ cup chopped red bell pepper

1 tablespoon minced fresh ginger

2 pounds peaches, peeled (see page 245), pitted, and diced (about 3½ cups)

½ cup fresh orange juice

¼ cup apple cider vinegar

½ cup packed light brown sugar

1½ teaspoons curry powder

½ teaspoon kosher salt

⅓ cup golden raisins

1 tablespoon chopped fresh cilantro

1. Heat the vegetable oil in a large saucepan over medium-high heat. Add the chile and cook, stirring, for 30 seconds. Add the onion and bell pepper and cook for 2 minutes, or until softened. Add the ginger and peaches; cook for 2 minutes. Stir in the orange juice, vinegar, brown sugar, and curry powder and mix well. Cover and bring to a boil. Reduce the heat to medium-low and cook for 10 minutes, or until the peaches are soft. Uncover and simmer, stirring occasionally, for 20 minutes, or until thickened. Stir in the salt, raisins, and cilantro. Transfer to a large bowl and let cool.

2. Store in an airtight container in the refrigerator for up to 3 weeks.

Peach Ketchup

Tangy and a tad bolder than standard ketchup, this homemade condiment gives any french fry or grilled meat extra oomph. We recommend Husk founder Sean Brock's Double Cheeseburger (see page 179) to go with.

Makes about 5 cups

Hands-on time: 1 hour

Total time: 1 hour plus cooling time

9 cups diced peeled (see page 245) peaches (about 5 pounds)

1 cup chopped sweet onion

3 garlic cloves, chopped

1½ cups packed brown sugar

½ cup distilled white vinegar

½ cup apple cider vinegar

2 tablespoons kosher salt

1 teaspoon finely ground black pepper

1 teaspoon dry mustard

½ teaspoon ground cloves

½ teaspoon ground allspice

½ teaspoon cayenne pepper

1. Combine the peaches, onion, garlic, and ¾ cup water in a large stainless-steel pot and bring to a simmer over medium heat. Simmer, stirring occasionally, for 10 minutes. Add the brown sugar, both vinegars, salt, black pepper, mustard, cloves, allspice, and cayenne. Bring back to a simmer and cook, stirring occasionally, until reduced by two-thirds, about 45 minutes.

2. Working in batches, carefully transfer the mixture to a blender or food processor and puree. Pass the ketchup through a fine-mesh sieve. Let cool to room temperature.

3. Store in an airtight container in the refrigerator for up to 4 weeks or in the freezer for up to 1 year.

Peach Fruit Leather

Why buy processed snacks from the store when you can make your own fresh fruit leather? By doing it yourself, you can adjust the sweetness, and even substitute honey or agave syrup for sugar. The fruit leather will keep in an airtight container for two to three weeks—although we somehow doubt it will sit around that long.

Makes 16 strips
Hands-on time: 20 minutes
Total time: 9 hours 20 minutes

3 cups sliced peeled (see page 245) peaches (about 3 medium)

Juice of 1 lemon

⅓ cup sugar, honey, or agave syrup, or to taste

1. Preheat the oven to 150° to 200°F (the lowest setting it will go). Line a half-sheet pan with a silicone baking mat.

2. In a blender or food processor, combine the peaches and lemon juice and puree until smooth. Taste for sweetness and add the sugar. Feel free to adjust the amount of sweetener based on your personal preference. Blend to combine.

3. Pour the peach puree onto the prepared pan and spread it evenly over the pan. Place on the center rack in the oven and bake for 6 to 8 hours, until the mixture is set and no longer tacky to the touch.

4. Remove from the oven and let cool to room temperature. Peel the fruit off the silicone mat and place on parchment paper or waxed paper. Use a pizza cutter to cut the fruit leather into strips. Peel the strips away from the paper and transfer them to an airtight container, layered between waxed paper or parchment paper.

Peach Mostarda

An Italian specialty, this piquant blend of candied peaches and spicy mustard is a wonderful accompaniment for grilled, roasted, and smoked meats, including sausages, duck, fish, and chicken, or an inviting platter of Italian charcuterie. Once ground, mustard seeds can become bitter over time, so we suggest using whole mustard seeds and grinding them in a spice mill yourself. The finished recipe will keep in your refrigerator for up to one week or your freezer for up to three months.

Makes about 3½ cups
Hands-on time: 25 minutes
Total time: 25 minutes

4 tablespoons mustard seeds

2½ cups distilled white vinegar

1 cup sugar

3 whole cloves

5 allspice berries

1 star anise pod

1 small cinnamon stick

1 teaspoon salt

3½ cups diced peeled (see page 245) peaches (3 to 4 medium)

1. Grind 2 tablespoons of the mustard seeds in a spice mill or crush them with a mortar and pestle. Set aside.

2. Combine the ground mustard seeds, the remaining 2 tablespoons mustard seeds, the vinegar, sugar, cloves, allspice, star anise, cinnamon stick, and salt in a medium saucepan. Bring to a boil over medium-high heat, reduce the heat to maintain a very low simmer and cook until reduced by half (this hydrates the mustard seeds and allows the spices to infuse them). Remove and discard the cinnamon stick, cloves, allspice, and star anise.

3. Put the peaches in a medium bowl. Pour the hot liquid over the peaches. Stir to combine. Let cool before refrigerating or freezing.

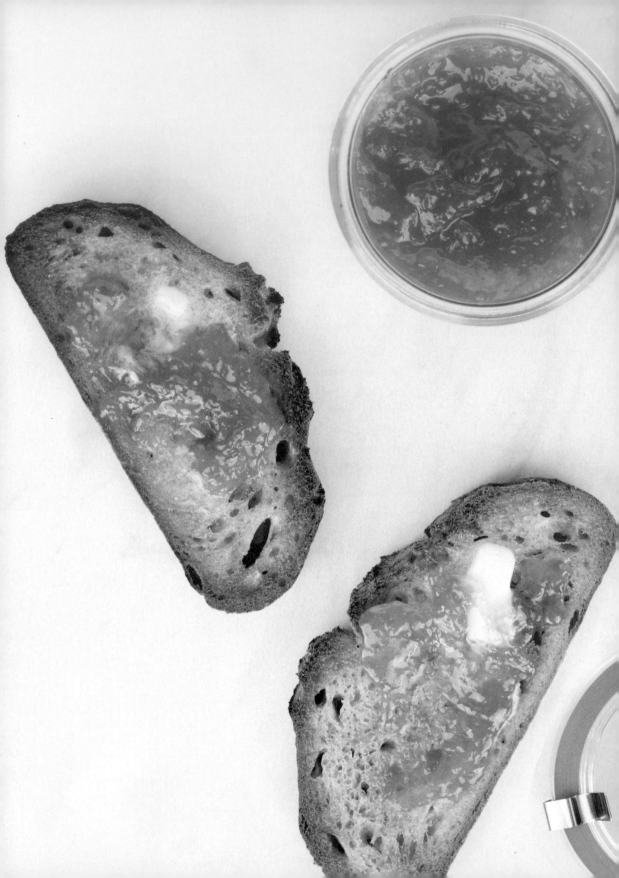

The Peach Truck
Signature Peach Jam

Essentially summer in a jar, this Peach Truck jam is one we searched for years to find. When we finally tasted this perfect recipe, we knew we had found the one. The star ingredient is peaches, not sugar, which we're especially proud of since it allows the queen of fruit to really shine. It's the ideal accompaniment to morning toast or a bagel, and a great way to enjoy the peach season's bounty all year long.

Makes 6 cups
Hands-on time: 40 minutes
Total time: 40 minutes

4 cups sugar

1 (1¾-ounce) package less-sugar/no-sugar-needed pectin

4½ cups peaches, peeled (see page 245), pitted, and finely chopped (about 5 medium)

3 tablespoons fresh lemon juice

2 teaspoons ascorbic acid (such as Fruit Fresh)

6 half-pint (8-ounce) jars with lids, sterilized

1. In a small bowl, mix together ½ cup of the sugar with the pectin.

2. Combine this mixture with the peaches, lemon juice, and ascorbic acid in a medium saucepan.

3. Bring this mixture to a hard boil over high heat (meaning the mixture will not stop bubbling when stirred) as you continuously stir. Slowly add the remaining 3½ cups sugar, a third at a time (so as not to reduce the temperature of the jam), until all the sugar is dissolved before adding more.

4. Once all the sugar is added, bring the mixture back to a boil for 1 minute. Remove from the heat, skim off any foam with a metal spoon, and carefully ladle into the sterilized jars, leaving ¼ inch of headspace. Wipe the jar rims of any jam and screw on the tops.

5. Prepare a hot water bath for canning. You can do this in a hot water bath canner or a large deep pot, with a cooling rack inside. Immerse the jars, on top of the rack, in the boiling water to cover 1 to 2 inches above the top of the jar lids. Cover the pot with a lid and bring to a boil. Process in the hot water bath for 10 minutes. Carefully remove the jars from the water; let stand at room temperature until cool.

Canned Peaches

Canning peaches is surprisingly easy: simply place the peeled peaches in one of the recipes for syrups provided below. Whichever option you choose, you'll be delighted to crack open a jar in the middle of winter and experience a burst of sunshine. You can eat these right out of the gate, add them to dessert or salad recipes, or broil them on the half in a pan with brown sugar and butter, a peachy take on classic baked apples.

Makes 8 cups
Hands-on time: 50 minutes
Total time: 50 minutes

8 or 9 medium peaches

LIGHT SYRUP

4 cups water

Juice of 1 lemon

2 cups sugar

HEAVY SYRUP

4 cups water

Juice of 1 lemon

3 cups sugar

HONEY SYRUP

3 cups water

2 cups honey

1. Blanch and peel soft, conditioned peaches according to the instructions on page 245. Halve and pit them, and place them in a bowl of ascorbic acid water to keep them from browning while preparing your jars.

2. Rinse the jars well and place them right side up on a rack in a water bath canner. Fill the canner and jars with water to 1 inch above the tops of the jars. Cover the canner, place on your burner, and heat water to just shy of boiling, about 180°F.

    Place the lids and rings in a saucepan and fill with water to 1 inch above the tops of the lids. Bring to a boil. Reduce the heat to low and leave the lids in simmering water while preparing the syrup.

3. Carefully remove the jars from water bath canner, pouring the water from inside the jars back into the canner. Place the peaches in the jars, cut side down. Combine the ingredients for your desired syrup in a medium saucepan. Bring to a boil over medium-high heat. Stir until the sweetener is dissolved. Fill the jars with the hot syrup, leaving ½ inch of headspace. Using a clean damp cloth, wipe the top rim of the jar to remove any residue. Remove lids from the hot water and place onto the jars.

4. Carefully lower the jars into the water bath canner, making sure the water is 1 inch above the tops of the jars. If not, add more hot water to cover. Cover and bring to a boil. Boil, covered, for 30 minutes, making sure the water is always covering the tops of the jars. Remove the jars carefully from the water and let cool for 12 hours on a dry towel or wire rack. The peaches may be stored in a cool, dry place away from direct sunlight for up to 1 year.

Frozen Peaches

One of the easiest ways to capture the taste of summer, freezing locks in the fresh peach flavor and gives you options for cooking and baking down the road.

Makes about 12 cups

Hands-on time: 20 minutes

Total time: 20 minutes plus freezing

8 to 10 medium peaches

Juice of 1 lemon

Sugar (½ teaspoon sugar for each peach)

1. Start with soft, conditioned peaches. Blanch and peel the peaches according to the instructions on page 245. Halve and pit the peaches.

2. Slice each peach half into 4 to 8 wedges and place them in a bowl. Add the lemon juice and ½ teaspoon sugar for each peach. The lemon juice will help prevent browning and the sugar will release the juices from the peaches, helping prevent air pockets when freezing. Toss to combine.

3. Transfer the peaches to a gallon-size zip-top freezer bag. We suggest measuring your peaches and writing the quantity and date on the outside of the bag. You can safely add 6 to 8 cups of peaches to each bag. Press any air out of the bag and seal.

4. Place the bag on a small baking sheet or cutting board (check to make sure it fits in your freezer first) and flatten the peaches. Place the baking sheet on a flat surface in the freezer and freeze until the peaches are solid.

5. Remove the baking sheet and store the peaches in the freezer until needed. (Freezing the bags flat will help you stack and store multiple bags, taking up less room in a crowded freezer.)

Peach Simple Syrup

This is one of the first recipes we tried when we started experimenting with peaches, and it's so cheerful and easy to make (only four ingredients, minutes to prepare) that it's fantastic to do as an activity with kids. The brilliantly colored syrup (thanks to the skin of the peaches), best kept refrigerated, is ideal for using throughout the year in desserts, cocktails, and iced tea.

Makes 4 cups

Hands-on time: 15 minutes (microwave) or 40 minutes (stovetop)

Total time: 15 minutes (microwave) or 40 minutes (stovetop)

4 medium peaches, pitted and cut into wedges

¼ cup fresh lemon juice

3 cups sugar

1 cup boiling water

MICROWAVE METHOD

1. This method is not only easy, but results in a fresh peach flavor. Place the peaches in a large microwave-safe glass bowl. Pour the lemon juice and sugar on top (do not stir) and cover very tightly with plastic wrap, wrapping it all the way around the bowl to seal in the steam while cooking. Microwave on high for 5 minutes.

2. Remove the bowl from the microwave and carefully remove the plastic so as not to burn yourself on the hot steam. Stir well. Cover and repeat the process until all the sugar has dissolved.

3. Strain the syrup through a fine-mesh sieve into a medium bowl to remove the solids. You can save the peaches to use as jam. Whisk in the boiling water and transfer the syrup to a jar. Allow to completely cool. Cover and refrigerate until needed, up to 1 month.

STOVETOP METHOD

1. Cooking on the stovetop will result in a syrup with more of a jammy flavor. Place the peaches, lemon juice, and boiling water in a medium saucepan. Add the sugar on top (do not stir). Bring to a simmer over medium-high heat. Reduce the heat to maintain a very low simmer, cover, and cook for 30 minutes. Resist the urge to stir while cooking, as this will break up the peaches. Remove from the heat.

2. Strain the syrup and bottle it as directed in step 3 of the microwave method.

Dried Peach Chips

These make a delicious snack on the go, especially because eating a fresh peach in the car can feel daunting. So grab your food dehydrator because once dried, the peaches have many uses. You can chop them up and add a few to cereal and granola, or cook and soften them on low heat in liquid (water, cider) until tender.

Makes about 5 cups

Hands-on time: 20 minutes

Total time: 15 hours 20 minutes

8 to 10 medium peaches

Juice of 1 lemon

1. Prior to handling the peaches, be sure to clean and sanitize your work area. Wash and scrub the peaches with a soft-bristled brush to remove any excess peach fuzz. Halve and pit the peaches.

2. Dehydrating whole halves will take much longer than thinner slices, so if desired, slice the halves into thinner uniform slices, 2 or 3 slices per half. The thinner the slices, the quicker they will dry, but keep them uniform so they will all dry at the same time.

3. Brush the cut surfaces of the peach slices with lemon juice to prevent browning and place them in a food dehydrator. Spread the slices evenly throughout the dehydrator to allow for adequate airflow. Dehydrate at 130° to 140°F for 10 to 15 hours. The peaches should be dry but still pliable when cool. Test a few pieces to see if they are ready before removing them from the dehydrator.

4. Once cool, store the dried peaches in an airtight container or zip-top bag in the freezer or refrigerator. If you're planning on storing them for any great length of time, place them in a large open pan after removing them from the dehydrator and let them air-dry for 10 to 12 days, tossing them occasionally. This will allow the moisture in the thickest areas of the slices to slowly dissipate.

5. While this recipe works best with a food dehydrator, you can also dry the peaches in your oven. Preheat the oven to its lowest setting. Thinly slice the peaches and place them on a rack over a baking sheet in the center of the oven. Prop the oven door open slightly with the handle of a wooden spoon to allow moisture to escape. Bake until the peaches are dry, but still pliable, 6 to 12 hours, depending on your oven.

Peach Vinegar

A vinegar lover's dream! Jessica's family believes vinegar is a miracle liquid: that it can aid with sore throats, digestive issues, and ailments of all kinds. This peach vinegar is a wonderful twist on this staple pantry item, one that brightens and brings depth to any recipe it touches. This simple recipe results in a refreshing fruity vinegar, delicious for dressings and marinades.

Makes 3 cups
Hands-on time: 15 minutes
Total time: 2 hours 45 minutes

2 cups sliced peeled (see page 245) peaches (about 2 medium)

2 cups distilled white vinegar

⅓ cup sorghum syrup, honey, or sugar

1. Place the peaches, vinegar, and sorghum syrup in a medium saucepan. Cover and bring to a boil over medium-high heat, watching carefully to avoid the mixture boiling over. Reduce the heat to maintain a simmer and cook for 10 minutes. Remove from the heat and let cool.

2. Transfer the mixture to a blender and blend until smooth.

3. Line a colander with cheesecloth and place it over a medium bowl. Pour the blended peach mixture into the cheesecloth-lined colander. Cover with a towel or plastic wrap and let it drain for 2 hours. Discard the solids and transfer the vinegar to a bottle for storage. The vinegar will keep in the refrigerator for up to 2 months.

Peach Hot Sauce

We put hot sauce on everything—sometimes in hopes that it will deter our kids from taking bites of our food, but so far, only one of our three kids doesn't like it. Peaches provide a sweet and sturdy base, balanced with the sharp, spicy flavors of habanero peppers (the heat can be turned up or down, depending on how many chiles you use). It is fantastic on everything from Grilled Grouper Tacos (page 154) to Fried Chicken Sliders (page 170).

When removing the stems and seeds from the habaneros, it's best to wear protective gloves and wash the cutting board and utensils afterward.

Makes 4 cups
Hands-on time: 25 minutes
Total time: 25 minutes

6 or 7 medium peaches, peeled (see page 245), pitted, and coarsely chopped

4 fresh habanero chiles, stemmed and seeded

1 cup packed light brown sugar

1½ cups distilled white vinegar

2 teaspoons sea salt

Pinch of freshly grated nutmeg

1. Combine the peaches, habaneros, brown sugar, and 1 cup of the vinegar in a large skillet and bring to a simmer over medium heat. Remove from the heat and let the mixture cool slightly.

2. Transfer the mixture to a blender and blend until very smooth. Pour the mixture into a medium saucepan, add the salt and nutmeg, and bring to a boil. Add the remaining ½ cup vinegar, bring back to a boil, and skim off any foam that rises to the top. Remove from the heat.

3. Carefully transfer the hot sauce to clean jars, let cool for 30 minutes, cover, and store in the refrigerator for up to 6 months.

Pickled Peaches

Pickled peaches feel both fun and fancy. Once made, they'll keep for months and are excellent eaten right out of the jar, but make an outstanding accompaniment to salads, sandwiches, and grilled and roasted meats—especially ham. We also like using the peaches and pickling syrup in salad dressings and shrub cocktails.

Makes 3 quarts

Hands-on time: 2 hours 10 minutes

Total time: 2 hours 10 minutes

14 medium peaches

2 tablespoons ascorbic acid (such as Fruit Fresh, to prevent browning)

10 cinnamon sticks

1½ teaspoons whole cloves, plus more for the jars

1½ teaspoons allspice berries

1½ cups apple cider vinegar

2½ cups distilled white vinegar

3½ cups sugar

½ teaspoon ground cardamom

1. Blanch the peaches following the instructions on page 245. Combine the ascorbic acid and 6 cups cold water in a separate large bowl. (You could also use ¼ cup fresh lemon juice or a few crushed chewable vitamin C tablets in place of the ascorbic acid.)

2. Place the peaches in the bowl of ascorbic acid water to keep them from browning.

3. Tie 4 of the cinnamon sticks, the cloves, and allspice in a piece of cheesecloth and place the bundle in a large saucepan. Add the apple cider vinegar, white vinegar, sugar, cardamom, and 2 cups water. Cover and bring to a simmer over medium-high heat. Simmer for 30 minutes to infuse the liquid with the spices. Increase the heat to high, bring the syrup to a rolling boil, and remove from the heat.

4. One at a time, remove the peach halves from the bowl of water and place them in the hot pickling syrup. Once all the peaches are in the pot, cover the pot and set it over low heat. Cook for 10 minutes, then raise the temperature to medium-high and cook for 5 minutes more, or until the liquid comes to a boil. Remove from the heat, cover, and let rest for 30 minutes.

5. Meanwhile, rinse three 1-quart jars well and place them right side up on a rack in a water bath canner. Fill the canner and jars with water to 1 inch above the tops of the jars. Cover the canner, place it on the burner, and heat the water to just shy of boiling, about 180°F. Place the lids and rings in a large saucepan and fill with water to 1 inch above tops of lids. Bring to a boil. Reduce the heat to low and leave the lids in simmering water.

6. Slowly remove the jars from the water bath canners, pouring the water from inside the jars back into the canner. Cover the canner. Use a slotted spoon to carefully remove the peaches from the syrup, one at a time, and place them cut side down in the prepared jars. Add 2 cinnamon sticks and 6 cloves to each jar. Fill each jar with the pickling syrup, leaving ½ inch of headspace. Using a clean damp cloth, wipe the top rim of the jars to remove any fruit or syrup. Remove the lids from the hot water and place onto the jars. Carefully lower the jars into the water bath canner, making sure the water is 1 inch above the tops of the jars. If not, add more hot water. Cover and bring to a boil. Continue to boil, covered, for 20 minutes, making sure the water is always covering the tops of the jars. Remove the jars carefully from the water and let cool for 12 hours on a dry towel or wire rack. The peaches may be stored in a cool, dry place away from direct sunlight for up to 6 months.

7. Excess pickling syrup can also be bottled and canned or refrigerated for use in dressings and cocktails. The peaches will keep for 6 months.

ACKNOWLEDGMENTS

To our parents, Greg and Barb Rose, and Paul and Debbie Nienaber: thank you for teaching us how to be the best versions of ourselves and for loving us through the seasons of life. We're so grateful for the examples that you've set for us and for Florence, Wyatt, and Rainier. Our love for you grows and grows.

Berta, we'll never forget receiving that first email from you and wondering: what could an agent from Beverly Hills possibly want with us? Three years later, we are so proud to see your vision come to pass. Thank you for believing in us and this project from the start.

To our core team: Rick, Meredith, and Michael. Each one of you works tirelessly to make the goals for The Peach Truck realities. You serve every customer, team member, and location with excellence, and for that we couldn't be more grateful. We so love ushering in the magic of summer alongside you. Thank you for your commitment and your trust.

Molly Creeden, thank you for helping us bring our words to paper. You patiently listened to us and helped us capture our story in such a special way.

To the Pearson Family: Thank you for faithfully growing peaches the right way for five generations, taking your craft seriously, and doing your work with excellence. We often say that y'all do 95 percent of the hard work, and it's our job to take that effort and get it over the finish line. We're humbled to partner with you to bring the Queen of Fruit to the masses.

To the McGehee Family: Without you, there wouldn't be The Peach Truck. Thank you for believing in us from the start. What began with thirty-two boxes of peaches on a Saturday in 2012 has turned into thousands of boxes every year. There's no one we want to make prouder.

Valerie Steiker, our editor, thank you for the endless support and belief in this book. We have felt so cared for during this process, and connecting with you over food and a vision has been a beautiful gift.

To everyone at Scribner, especially Nan Graham, Colin Harrison, Roz Lippel, Brian Belfiglio, Jaya Miceli, Sally Howe, Kara Watson, Abigail Novak, Ashley Gilliam, and Mia Crowley-Hald, who supported this project from the beginning and helped make it a wonderful reality. And to Jen Wang, our interior designer, whose designs brought this cookbook gorgeously to life.

Our Cookbook Team:

Torie Cox, recipe developer and food stylist, there are no words for the treasure you are. Thank you for your commitment to this process, and your focus and precision at every step. Your skills are incredible and we are fortunate to have had you on this team.

Jamie Bayer, digital tech, we didn't know we needed you until you were there, and then we couldn't live without you. You are talented beyond belief, and working alongside you was such a joy.

Mindi Shapiro, prop stylist, your eye for unique dishes is excellent. We are grateful to have been able to use your treasures to display our culinary works.

Victoria Clemmons, assistant chef, if ever there was an ideal person to round out a team, it is you! We can't believe we were gifted with your presence. Your work ethic and camaraderie are such a joy to encounter.

Eliesa Johnson, photographer, words cannot express how grateful we are to you for capturing our world in such a beautiful, meaningful way. Thank you for your unending effort and commitment to this project, and your love and support of us as fellow entrepreneurs. Your friendship is one that we will always treasure!

To the brilliant Nashville chefs and restaurants who contributed to this project: Sean Brock, Rebekah Turshen, Teresa Mason, Kayla May, Craig Schoen, Crystal Luna-Bogan, Julia Van Winkle, Tandy Wilson, Jeni Britton Bauer, Margot McCormick, Lisa Donovan, Matt Bolus, Edley's BBQ, & Burger Up. We are so humbled that with all the demands on your time, you took a moment to share your recipes here. Thank you for feeding us and this precious community that we share.

And finally, our deepest appreciation is owed to the people and places who have helped us build The Peach Truck; from friends who supported us in our early years, to our loyal customers, and the many host locations who allow us to spread the peach love. What a beautiful journey it's been.

INDEX

Note: Page references in **bold** indicate photographs.

ABOUT THE AUTHORS

J essica N. Rose and Stephen K. Rose, the cofounders of The Peach Truck, have been featured in national media from the *Today* show to *Food & Wine* to *Southern Living*. They live in Nashville, Tennessee, with their three children.